POEMS and SONGS of the PRESIDENTS of the 20TH CENTURY

A 100 year collection by
John Kermit Kerr

****

Paintings by
R. Bruce Johnston

Copyright © 2016 John Kermit Kerr
All rights reserved
First Edition

PAGE PUBLISHING, INC.
New York, NY

First originally published by Page Publishing, Inc. 2016

ISBN 978-1-68289-488-0 (pbk)
ISBN 978-1-68289-489-7 (digital)
ISBN 978-1-68289-490-3 (hardcover)

The poems are fictional works by the author.

The paintings are by Bruce Johnston who retains ownership of the paintings. Photographs are from publicly available sources, primarily *Wikipedia*. The image of the American flag was licensed from istockphoto.com

Printed in the United States of America

CONTENTS

A BRIEF EXPLANATION OF THE COLLECTED POEMS		5
INTRODUCTION TO THE POEMS		7
William McKinley	Ohio	12
Theodore Roosevelt	New York	36
William Howard Taft	Ohio	58
Woodrow Wilson	New Jersey	74
Warren G. Harding	Ohio	96
Calvin Coolidge	Massachusetts	106
Herbert Hoover	California	114
Franklin D. Roosevelt	New York	128
Harry S. Truman	Missouri	138
Dwight David Eisenhower	Kansas	156
John F. Kennedy	Massachusetts	168
Lyndon B. Johnson	Texas	182
Richard M. Nixon	California	198
Gerald Ford	Michigan	204
Jimmy Carter	Georgia	212
Ronald Reagan	California	224
George H. W. Bush	Texas	244
William Jefferson Clinton	Arkansas	266
A READER'S GUIDE TO THE POEMS		284

A BRIEF EXPLANATION OF THE COLLECTED POEMS

*George Cortelyou gave Robert the old leather box,
believed to have belonged to Ulysses Grant. Robert used the box to collect
campaign buttons, cartoons, poems and other items of interest.*

Three men collected poems written by or about the eighteen presidents of the twentieth century. The first of these men was named Robert whose deceased father had served with McKinley at Antietam during the Civil War. After his father died, Robert secured a menial job at the Executive Mansion and moved from Ohio to Washington. He began work in the stables and later found work in the main house.

Robert was befriended by George Cortelyou, William McKinley's personal secretary, who later became a senator from Ohio. Cortelyou took an interest in Robert. He gave the young man an old leather box, said to have belonged to President Ulysses Grant. He told Robert to collect odds and ends that no one wanted, such as ticket stubs, campaign buttons or letters that were to be thrown away. He pointed out that people would send the president poems from time to time, and he should keep those he found interesting. He also mentioned that the president had written several poems. Robert followed Cortelyou's advice and began his collection.

Following McKinley's assassination in 1901, Robert remained an employee in the Executive Mansion. He served a total of six presidents: McKinley, Theodore Roosevelt, William Howard Taft, Woodrow Wilson, Warren G. Harding and Calvin Coolidge. He retired after Coolidge left office.

Robert was succeeded by his son James who inherited the leather box. James continued the tradition of keeping interesting odds and ends and poems in the old leather box. In time, James served six presidents before he retired. They were Herbert Hoover, Franklin Roosevelt, Harry Truman, Dwight Eisenhower, John Kennedy and Lyndon Johnson. When James retired, he was succeeded by his son John.

John continued to work in the White House, as had his father and grandfather. While there, John served Richard Nixon, Gerald Ford, Jimmy Carter, Ronald Reagan, George H. W. Bush and William Clinton.

John maintained the tradition of collecting odds and ends, but he tended to keep poems and press clippings more often.

INTRODUCTION TO THE POEMS

An Old Man lies in his bed in a nursing home and welcomes a visitor who has come to see him. The Old Man was born in 1901 and is nearing his final days. He lived in Washington DC and knew Robert, James and John well. His visitor asks for him to recount stories of the presidents whom he knew and share stories of the three men who worked in the White House.

The Old Man Receives a Visitor

My caregivers watched your car arrive,
crunching through the trees on the gravel drive.
Outside, it is cold for this time of year,
and I am pleased that you found us here.

I am in the final stage of progressive care,
worthless inventory in a wheelchair.
Here the customers never get well, and the home
has a mixture of smells—strong disinfectants and
bodily waste, striking visitors like a slap in the face.

While you are here, try hard to tolerate the foul
odor. It will never abate. So let us spend our time in
conversation and postpone the time of my cremation.

Draw closer to me for I am older than anyone
you have ever known. My eyesight is poor, and
no longer am I able to stand without my cane.

Getting old is the better of choices, so I am told, but
being almost deaf will make me helpless to Death's
embraces, when he decides my life is finished.

JOHN KERR

Let me move to the point of our meeting.
You requested to interview me before the
sands empty from my hour glass.

You want me to out race Father Time and share
my stories of American presidents of the twentieth
century ending last year with William Clinton,
all the way back to William McKinley.

I was born in 1901, a few weeks before McKinley
was murdered in Buffalo, so I never knew him
personally, but he sent my father a warm letter of
congratulations on my birth, drafted by our family
friend George Cortelyou, with bold predictions
that I would lead a long and useful life.

I was raised near the Executive Mansion. I ate there
often and played on the lawn because of my father's
law connection. One of my friends there was named
Robert, who shared his lunch from the kitchen.

Our friendship grew, and it lasted throughout
his years of service to six presidents. After
those years, he was depleted, worn out,
and needed to restore his health.

He retired and transferred his work responsibilities
to his son James when Herbert Hoover came to
the White House in the 1930s. Please listen to
these words of poetry written in the twentieth
century by and for eighteen presidents.

They were collected by three servants, who worked
in the White House. Their careers spanned a period
of a hundred years and gave them the opportunity
to observe the daily lives of those they served.

The first named Robert began working in
the stables and the White House garden.
Soon he became friends with George
Cortelyou, William McKinley's secretary,

who helped him get a job in the kitchen,
his first job in the Executive Mansion.

Cortelyou gave Robert an old leather box, said
to be where Grant kept his liquor when he was
president. "Keep mementos such as letters, essays,
poetry and prose in it, or photographs of his wife,
Ida, taken with this new Brownie camera."

He told Robert, "Perhaps in the future you
will look back on these days with pleasure."
Robert continued working for thirty more
years, running errands, making coffee, carrying
messages, and eavesdropping when Congressmen
were drinking. He served tea to Ida McKinley
and helped the maids hang laundry.

Roosevelt took an interest in his reading, quizzing
him at length on his understanding of a text and the
author's intent, or what a particular passage meant.
Often Taft used Robert as a caddy whose task
was to set the ball on a tee for Taft's substantial
girth prevented him from bending or made
him light headed when he tried to rise.

Once Robert helped Taft from his bathtub when
he was jammed and stuck from the suction of his
massive frame and weight, helpless and held captive.

For Wilson, he carried important messages between the White House and branches of the military during the Great War, serving by riding in a chauffeured car.

Often Harding invited men for a poker game, and many prominent business leaders came for the pleasure of losing to Harding. We let him think he was winning. Robert served cigars, kept rye glasses full, and smoking trays empty of ashes. Even though it was during prohibition, Harding drank rye with no inhibition.

The Coolidges enjoyed sailing on Sundays, so Robert worked the lines and in the galley. He sailed with a Potomac breeze to the end of the 1920s.

The old leather box contained sixty poems and songs by the presidents when Robert retired after thirty years of service. Robert gave the box to his son who was given a job by Herbert Hoover in 1929.

When Robert retired, we gave a reception and asked if he would read from the papers of his presidential poetry collection. He agreed, and it was a splendid evening.

The poems helped us recall our history of struggle and achievement, triumphs in war, economic uncertainty, scientific and social advancement, soaring hopes and personal tragedies.

A new electrically powered phonograph had been installed which we used to record his remarks. His speech was transcribed and preserved, thanks to this technical innovation, and is an important piece of oral history and the fabric of our nation.

The poems, often in the author's own hand, reveal emotions of joy and sorrow, disappointment and suppressed anger. They bring each author out of the shadows, speaking to us from a receding time, recounting days of deep sadness, psychic pain, or unfettered happiness.

The Old Man then played a recording made at Robert's retirement party recounting Robert's years in the White House.

A Reception in the White House (Recorded in January 1929)

President and Mrs. Coolidge, Dear Friends, Fellow Staff and Colleagues, tonight ends my years of service here. I am pleased you are here tonight and deeply moved. You do me great honor with your presence as I read from poems of six presidents.

Tonight, when I stood behind the curtain
listening to that warm introduction,
I recalled the evening we turned the calendar to 1900.
The first was a Monday, and it was cold. Brass on
the carriages gleamed like gold from my efforts
that began before dawn. Fires had been lit in the
kitchen ovens, and smells of coffee and frying
bacon Drifted over the frost-covered lawn.
I had been told to have the horses ready in case
the president took an early ride in the morning air
before breakfast. I was fifteen years old in 1900.
My father died when I was twelve. He had served
with McKinley at Spring Mountain and in battles at
Winchester and Antietam. Shortly after the death of
my father, an unpleasant man married my mother.
He made it clear that I was no longer welcome in the
house, nor was my younger brother who was taken in
by a spinster aunt who did not have room for another.
An uncle took me from that dreadful place and
found me temporary work and a space for me to
sleep in a grocery store beneath a dry good's table on

the floor. My mother had acted out of desperation,
but I can still feel the pain of her rejection.
My uncle wrote a letter of petition, a poorly
structured composition, to McKinley on my behalf,
asking for work for me. Then we began waiting. After
a long delay, an answer came, and in a few days, I was
on the train headed from Ohio to Washington where
I would be working in a mansion. On the eve of
America's century, I headed east to meet my destiny.
They put me to work cleaning out stables,
and in time, I learned to groom the horses.
I learned to hitch a team to a carriage and
load the wagons and stow the luggage.
In time, a job became available, which took me
out of the stables and into the main house as a
servant. I moved from a stall to the basement. The
head steward gave me new clothes, trained me
well, and bought me new shoes. He made sure I
was well tailored, taught me etiquette, and to act
cultured. Over time I worked as a courier, servant,
valet, messenger, and caterer. Cortelyou was my
first of three mentors who taught me diction and
proper manners. He taught me to smile and how
to be helpful and the political art of being tactful.
A gift from Cortelyou is this antique box with
brass locks and handles and a sleek leather
covering. He gave it to me, suggesting I keep
Mementos, programs, ticket stubs, poems, letters,
campaign buttons, and anything that might be a
reminder of the people I met in my work here.

WILLIAM MCKINLEY
President 1898-1901

Robert Introduces the McKinley Poems

Robert describes a meeting with Cornelius Vanderbilt,
Andrew Carnegie, John D. Rockefeller, and J. P.
Morgan hosted by Mark Hannah to raise money for
McKinley's reelection campaign. As Vanderbilt departs
he hands Robert notes he kept in the form of a
Poem by Mark Hannah. In receiving the poem
From Vanderbilt, Robert establishes the tradition
Of keeping presidential poetry.

We start with Mark Hannah's Modern Campaign
Given to me by Commodore Vanderbilt
On his way to a private train
Following a meeting with Mark Hannah.

Then we will endure Cline's Hurricane
That struck Galveston Island in the Gulf.
Then I will follow it with a sonnet of pain
Torn from the heart of Ida McKinley.

I will read an elegy of sadness,
Spoken by Cortelyou at the service honoring
President McKinley.

We will read selections that bear witness
To the confession of an act of madness.

POEMS AND SONGS OF THE PRESIDENTS OF THE 20TH CENTURY

We will conclude the evening with a poem,
Part of a larger, now lost volume
About Antietam and South Mountain
Where McKinley fought in the Civil War.

Soldier, president, son of Ohio,
We salute you, American hero

One morning I was told to look my best.
At two, we would receive important guests
Whom Mr. Hannah had asked to raise
The necessary funds to help defray
Costs of telling our candidate's story.
He said, "The fuel of election is money."

We were told to expect financiers
And industrialists, men without peers
In their respective fields of endeavor.
The oil titan J. D. Rockefeller
Was surrounded by his security
Men. Agents of Andrew Carnegie

Raising money for McKinley.
Andrew Carnegie, J. P. Morgan, Cornelius Vanderbilt, and John D. Rockefeller are pressured by Mark Hannah for contributions to McKinley's reelection campaign. McKinley observes the proceedings through a window. Accompanies the modern campaign of 1899.

Accidentally merged their wagons
With of those of financier J. P. Morgan.
In the confusion men began shouting,
Their teams bolting in a storm of cursing.
When Commodore Vanderbilt arrived late,
His men drove his carriage through a gate
At the rear of the mansion. I escorted
Him to Mr. Hannah who was angered
By the scene out front and discouraged
By the way the arrivals were managed.

The meeting started and was in progress
When I was told to fetch oils and canvass,
And then locate the White House artist
To record the day America's richest men
Put large resources behind McKinley's
Election campaign with money pledges.

Commodore Vanderbilt departed first
And said without my asking, "Coerced,
Threatened, my arm has been twisted.
There is no way I could have resisted.
I have documented their subtle threats
Against my corporations and assets."
He handed me scraps of notes on paper,
And leaning over, said in a whisper,
"Keep this poem a secret and well hidden
In case there is trouble, a crime of passion,
Or an act like an assassination.
Now fetch my men and hitch my wagon.
I must leave this place as fast as I dare
And hope to escape their treacherous snare.

So Commodore Vanderbilt departed,
And this is how my collection started.
I put the poem in the old leather box,
Softened by oil, sealed with brass locks.

POEMS AND SONGS OF THE PRESIDENTS OF THE 20TH CENTURY

McKinley ran on his record of prosperity and victory in 1900, winning easy reelection over Bryan.

The Modern Campaign of 1899

A cordial welcome to this meeting hall.
If you require refreshment, I will call
A servant to make your stay more pleasant.
Perhaps tea, champagne, or pressed pheasant—
Anything you require, please let us provide
Such as we meet to discuss and decide
Vital issues that press us and threaten
The peace and serenity of our nation.
The president knows that we are meeting
And sends his warmest heartfelt greetings.
You four have supported our noble cause
Away from limelight and raucous applause.
Before we start, may I offer cigars?
Finest quality I am told: prewar.

So our mission today is to extend
Our appreciation and recommend
Extended uses of your generous

Contributions supporting our purpose.
In this first term, our record is spotless

For total support of American business.
We have been a wise trustee
Of a strengthening national economy.
On issues you like we remain steadfast,
Allowing no legislation passed
That might upset or ultimately spoil
Antitariff, benevolent trust, or oil,
Or any issue that we think adverse,
Or harm our mutual plans for commerce.
And with the destruction of the *US Maine*
We won a popular war with toothless Spain.
Two hemispheres have felt our naval power.
We can say easily that now is our hour.

In spite of our progress, this mixed stew
Of citizenry shows to you
A distracting, dark side of our public
Not guided or grounded by moral ethic.
Some say that only the very richest
Benefit from the benevolent trusts.
The words of a misguided fanatic
Preach a doctrine that could end in tragic
Events that could halt hard-won breakthroughs
For each complex financial issue.
Vapors of this simmering cauldron
Smell of mayhem and assassination.

Gentlemen, I am pleased to explain
Our need for funds for a modern campaign.
It is no secret that to reach the country
We need effective political machinery.
And to run a campaign that is vibrant,
We need your support to serve as lubricant.

Our task will be to keep him in Canton
Making his victory appear as a foregone
Conclusion. He will carry the party's torch,
Welcoming visitors from his front porch.
We will show him with the victor's garland

While serving as the national husband,
A strong firm hand guiding us on a calm
Course, well above the campaign maelstrom.
We know that we must assure our message
Gets beyond yellow journalistic verbiage.
Measured parts of your thoughtful largess
Will go to securing a favorable press.
We will secure amenable journalists
To attack Bryan like a swarm of locusts.
The press will write stories favorable
To us, portraying our man's high moral
Character, developing contrasts with true
Descriptions of each candidate's virtues.

Across the land we show steadfast purpose,
Guided by our political compass.
Judicious use of your generous funds
Will allow creation of favorable legends
Attacking our opponent with articles
That rake his position and stifle
His message with devastating lampoons
Through widespread use of political cartoons.

Yes, I see that I have exceeded my time.
Length of speech is often a fault of mine.
To summarize, anything you might provide
Can give us an electoral landslide.
As you make your way to your carriage
Please notice a new painting many judge
Exceptional. It is heroic Dewey
Securing the Philippines with our brave navy.

Ah yes, your men and carriages are here,
But one last important thought for your ear.
We consider it our sacred duty
To protect your specific industry.

Our best wishes to you, Mr. Morgan.
Pleasant journey; our offer is a bargain.
And farewell to you, Mr. Rockefeller.
We think of you as our standard bearer.
And Godspeed to you, Mr. Carnegie.

I put in your hamper some Scottish whiskey.
In truth, I feel discernable guilt
For missing Commodore Vanderbilt
As he hurried in his quest to go.
Look up, see who watches from the window.

Hannah

* * * *

A Tragic Hurricane on the Gulf Coast

Once Mrs. McKinley set a departure
Date, we had two days to get the house clean
Of files, correspondence, trash, and clutter
Before the Roosevelts arrived on the scene.
Several of us were assigned the task
Of disposing trash. With no one to ask
If documents were important,
We were forced to use our best judgment.

From a file marked Cline Nineteen Hundred,
Letters and a sestina were added
To my growing literary collection.
Isaac Cline was head of the weather station
When a hurricane struck without warning
Causing widespread death and devastation.
In Washington we did not comprehend
The extent of the Texas tragedy
Until his sestina let us understand.

Robert

* * * *

The Hurricane of 1900 at Galveston, Texas

As physical forces we call nature
Bear down on sunlit Galveston Island,
A dark and deep blue mysterious sea
Helps build the beginnings of a hurricane,

Sending from the east a peculiar wind
And launching at land an unusual tide.

Unable to restrain the rising tide,
Indifferent to man's place in nature,
An unrestrained force of deadly wind
Slams against the unsuspecting island,
Bringing sudden death by the hurricane,
As no wall could hold back the swelling sea.

An unrelenting powerful surge of the sea
Swallowed our hope to fight rising tide.
Manmade things were destroyed by nature.
Our station, destroyed by hurricane
Strength winds, was swept off the island
And lost completely in the howling wind.

Homes were blown apart by the wind,
And lives were lost in the inescapable sea.
Little exit from Galveston Island
Was possible because the record tide
Provided by an uncaring nature
Brought us great misery from the hurricane.

Embedded in the eye of the hurricane,
Tossed about in inconsistent wind
Are catastrophic results of nature.
Sometimes calm, sometimes violent, the sea
Pressed to landfall with its deadly tide,
And with a surge, struck Galveston Island.

So ended countless lives on the island,
Laid low by hubris and a hurricane.
Signs ignored, such as the rising tide,
Overlooked, the velocity of the wind,
Warnings from Cuba regarding the sea:
Arrogance versus the forces of nature.

Tercet

Nature's task was not done on the island.
The sea pulled back, and the hurricane

Left a dying wind and receding tide.

Sestina of Isaac Cline
September 8, 1900

* * * *

A Tragedy in Buffalo

George B. Cortelyou gave me a copy
Of President McKinley's eulogy
When he returned on the funeral train
With the president's mortal remains.

We laid him in the East Room for his farewell
With a rose from the garden in his lapel.

Good-bye, son of Ohio.
We will shield your widow
From the tragedy in Buffalo.

I kept the eulogy in Grant's old box
Guarded by padded brass locks.

Robert

* * * *

Eulogy of William McKinley

Soldier, President, Son of Ohio
We salute you, American Hero.

Today, we brought you to this Rotunda,
Presented in state to be bid farewell
By citizens from all social strata,
Joined by sorrow in a common hell.

We sat most of the day near your casket.
We must display you until tomorrow.
Crushing grief covers us in a blanket
Of unspeakable despair and sorrow.

Early today a military band
Led the procession to City Hall
Playing the funeral march of Chopin.
As we arrived, rain began to fall.

With the Exposition in Buffalo
All manner of people from the country
Are here including Chief Geronimo
Who brought, with other chiefs, this eulogy:

The rainbow of hope is out of the sky.
Heavy clouds hang about us.
Tears wet the ground of the tepees.
The Chief of the Nation is dead.
Farewell.

Our new century lies in that coffin.
Tomorrow we travel to Washington.
You were to be our great transition.
Instead, we are headed back to Canton.

In the years ahead, few will remember
Respect Abroad was your call to duty.
Uniting us all, you were our leader.
Prosperity At Home is your legacy.

Soldier, President, Son of Ohio
We salute you, American Hero.

George B. Cortelyou
September 16, 1901

* * * *

Caring for Ida McKinley

Mrs. McKinley's health was an issue
During her time as mistress of the House.
She suffered from a variety of
Ailments and disorders. Often she was
Bed ridden with painful migraine headaches,
In constant fear for her husband's safety.

Mister Ike Hoover was the chief usher
Of the White House. Under his watchful eye
I was allowed to work on kitchen
Detail during special dinners or when
Extra staff was required to serve and
Remove dishes and tableware. During State
Department receptions and dinners,
My assigned task was to help with the
Coffee service after the desert course.

Once I escorted Mrs. McKinley
Back to her room during a State dinner.
She was not feeling well and needed help
Walking the return trip to her quarters.
After that occasion, she would request I
Run errands or perform small tasks for her.

The President was attentive to her.
After she left, I found a pitiful
Sonnet among her discarded papers.

Robert

* * * *

Ida's Sonnet

The lights in my eyes signal a migraine.
Draw the curtains and close the windows.
It is my prudent action to remain sane
Living in darkness and gloomy shadows.

In this way I hold back my miseries
And secure some measure of relief
From one of my numerous maladies
Attributed by my doctors to grief.

If only some physician could rescue
Me from this enclosed, nightmarish cell,
My life could restart or begin anew
And break free to escape this living hell.

I was free once of this foul depression.
That was before we buried our children.

Ida

* * * *

They Executed McKinley's Assassin

It was a time of economic stress
For many persons, and social unrest
Boiled up among the dispossessed.

Anarchy and violence preached by devils
As methods of destroying the evils
Of capitalistic societies.
Arsonists, bomb throwers—people with no
Legitimate complaints mixed in with
Persons who saw great injustices
In our country and used them for their own
Nefarious and selfish purposes.

Leon Czolgosz was a troubled soul
Under the influence of an anarchist
Named Emma Goldberg who inspired
Dark acts of sedition and lawlessness.
She and many like her conspired
To cause acts of terror in class warfare.

Czolgosz offered no defense for himself.
He had volunteered his martyrdom.
What is in the mind of a terrorist
That tricks him into believing that good
Can issue from an act of destruction?

The terrorist is nothing more than an
Unwitting tool of a stronger mind
Bent upon a course of evil action.
Camouflaged evil is still evil.
The terrorist is a blind accomplice.

* * * *

Ballade of Leon Czolgosz

It took courage to be an anarchist
And formulate a great act of treason.
Then you taught me to be a good Marxist.
Hearing your speech, my brain became molten,
Aflame with desire to be the gunman.
All kings and rulers are our enemy.
I would be an extension of the weapon.
Our enemy is all authority.

It was my hope the movement could harvest
The timely deaths of more than one sovereign,
Thereby launching a furious tempest
To destroy completely obscene mansions
With expert use of the arsonist's bomb.
An organized state is tyranny.
Some day we will join in equal union.
Our enemy is all authority.

Fair wages are denied by the richest
Who are society's malignant lesion.
The greedy deny freedom through their trusts.
There is no sense of time in this dungeon,
But I hear them building my coffin.
Our most dangerous foes are the wealthy.
I neither seek nor expect a pardon.
Our enemy is all authority.

Emma Goldberg—our inspired Russian,
You have explained a great mystery.
Now I go to my electrocution.
Our enemy is all authority.

Sung on September 14, 1901
by Leon Czolgosz

✶ ✶ ✶ ✶

My Father Gave Me This from the Civil War

My father told me very little of
His time in the Civil War, believing
It best that he put his mind on living
In the future rather than living in the past.
After he died, my uncle gave me a
Section of a long, narrative saga

Which eventually was placed in
My old leather box. The early portion
Of the poem, and the last of the stanzas
Are missing. The section which I have here
Recounts the arrival in Washington
Of McKinley, his brief time in wartime
Washington, a temporary march to
The south to guard access to the city,
And then a glorious march to Maryland.

At South Mountain, just beyond Frederick,
His regiment pushed rebel forces
Out of Fox's Gap with General Hayes
In command. President Lincoln enjoyed
The victory and urged the Union forces
To pursue the rebel army with all
Their force and destroy them, if possible.

In command, General George McClellan
Brought his numerically powerful force
To Antietam where General Lee
Occupied the high ground. The next day,
September seventeenth, became the largest
Day of loss of American lives in
The history of our noble country.

Twenty-two thousand soldiers fell that day.
It was senseless slaughter on both sides of
The conflict. McClellan could have won the
Day but refused to bring up reserves
At the critical part of the fighting.

This narrative poem describes the role of

McKinley at South Mountain and Antietam.
It is my hope that someday the complete
Narrative will be recovered and read.

Robert

✷✷✷✷

Stone Mountain and Antietam Washington— August 24, 1862

Five thousand men packed in railroad cars
Arrived at dawn at Washington Station.
Baltimore and Ohio crew pushed us out
Into oppressive heat and mass confusion.

We fetched our baggage as best we could
And formed our ranks in parade formation.
Our regimental band played patriotic tunes,
Guiding us to the Executive Mansion.

Uncle Abraham spoke quietly from the porch,
And talked of many things the men hold dear.
He spoke of country, family, and home.
So we thanked him with a hearty cheer.

For two days we remained in Washington,
Engulfed by weather that was hot and damp,
But we were nourished with delicious food,
Prepared by ladies nearby our camp.

The city was a welcome diversion for our men.
Each afternoon we toured the important sites.
We saw constant reminders of this war,
Bringing frightful dreams and sleepless nights.

Had someone said a future President
Was among us and on our cooking crew,
We'd never have guessed it was McKinley
Peeling carrots and onions for our stew.

We were ready to leave on the third day.

Our task was to protect a southern route.
We were happy to leave the Capitol.
At the General's command, our men moved out.

Fort Ramsey and Fort Buffalo—August 26, 1862

Our regiment crossed the Potomac Bridge
Taking our easy time and marching slow
Beyond Falls Church and south to Upton's Hill
To guard Fort Ramsey and Fort Buffalo.

During three days of leisurely marching,
Rumors flew to our camp from near and far
That Lincoln was planning a battle
To end this terrible war.

As we guarded the Forts near Upton's Hill,
Sound of distant cannon meant no denying
That a second Bull Run was under way now,
And men were falling, wounded and dying.

Guarding the forts, we had little to do,
But watch fearful troops trudge west to the roar,
As they shared the road with east-bound wagons
Loaded with men no longer fit for war.

Rumor at the Fort was that General Lee
Was seeking a suitable location
To engage us in a final battle
That would set the future of the nation.

We speculated endlessly on our future roles,
When and where we would enter the fray.
Were we doomed to stay at Fort Buffalo
And miss the glory of the final days?

We heard that Uncle Abraham had his
Fill of endless recruiting and marching.
He gave McClellan specific orders
To prepare to fight and stop parading.

Then we heard Ole Abe told the General to

*Find the whereabouts of General Lee,
And seek his army out to engage him,
And destroy the Confederate army.*

Each soldier had his favorite leader,
And each had his own nomination
For the best tactician during combat
To lead us into our Armageddon.

We received our orders in a week.
The news had come directly from Lincoln.
Lee was on a northern march to Maryland,
Where we would teach the Rebels a lesson.

Our troops were assigned to Ambrose Burnside
And marched at the head of the Union Army.
We were to march to Frederick, Maryland
And lead the Army with honor and glory.

South Mountain—September 14, 1862

We marched through Washington to Frederick,
Past verdant pastures in pleasant weather.
Encouraged and cheered along the road
Our spirits soared high, our hearts grew braver.

Nearing Frederick, we saw the enemy.
It was a detachment of their cavalry.
We pushed forward; they retreated.
We moved in without firing a volley.

In town, we received a joyous welcome
As we marched into the Courthouse Square.
Old men blessed us; women wept as they
Waved their handkerchiefs in the air.

The rebels were a mile forward up ahead.
Keeping a safe distance, we followed.
We knew our futures lay in front of us
As we marched up the National Road.

The National Road led us to South Mountain.

Confederates shot at us to harass
Our slow advance toward their positions
Where they held and guarded each hilly pass.

Led by the 23rd, Scannon's brigade arrived.
We were to charge the rebels at point-blank,
Strike and roll them back against their battle line
At Fox's Gap, protecting our right flank.

By Sunday morn, we were in position.
Endless waiting made us scared to death.
Rancid bile and fear rose in our throats.
Most of us could not speak or catch our breath.

Our officers formed us in the woods
With bayonets fixed for grisly wounds.
We lined up, cheered, and charged
Across a hundred yards of open ground.

A thunderous roar from behind a fence
Caught us as we charged from the sheltered wood.
We kept running to meet the enemy
And bayonet them wherever they stood.

The brave ones kept on fighting to their death.
Some tried to surrender as a last action.
Our hearts filled with murderous rage
We gutted them all in mass destruction.

General Hayes called for a second charge,
And as he commanded the men to go
A blast of fragments from a minie ball
Hit him, crushing his arm above the elbow.

Dying and dead were stacked like firewood
Blocking our way on a path so muddy
We could do nothing but toss them aside
To move our wagons and artillery.

A final charge secured the battlefield.
Their main force had withdrawn during the night.
Leaving minimal troops across the pass

Lee had selected Sharpsberg for the fight.

Our regiment spent the night with the dead.
At sunrise, we fed the men and took count.
Detaching a detail to bury the slain
We followed Lee on a direct route.

Our victory was purchased at great cost.
Word spread that Lincoln had wired McClellan,
God bless you all and all with you, now go,
Destroy the rebel army if you can.

Lee had made a bold and strategic move
And outmaneuvered George McClellan.
He was digging on the heights near Sharpsberg
By Dunker's Church and the creek Antietam.

* * * *

Antietam Creek, Maryland September 17, 1862

Next morning, we followed Bobby Lee.
He was forming his lines at Antietam.
His army established an advantage there,
While our Generals worked on new plans.

We had larger numbers in our army.
Our artillery had more destructive power,
But Lee's choice of the battleground gave
Them an advantage over our armor.

Lee was above on top of a clear ridge,
From where his troops were easily aligned.
For quarters, McClellan picked a house
With only a partial view of the line.

We spent the afternoon making demonstrations,
Engaged in precombat feigning.
By nightfall, we were emotionally spent.
We were in place at two in the morning.

The battle opened on our right flank.

Cannon thundered before day's first light.
Men died by the hundreds before sunrise,
Slaughtered, as they began to fight.

The open fields were made for destruction.
Our staff tried to estimate the cost.
By day's end, 10,000 Confederates
And 12,000 Union men would be lost

The Bridge—Afternoon, September 17, 1862

We deployed on the Army's far left flank
To secure a crossing at Rohrbach's bridge.
The woods above teemed with Confederates.
They stared down at us from a wooded ridge.

General Burnside ordered charges
In attempt to secure the other side,
But each charge across was nothing more than
Savage butchery and mass suicide.

George McClellan was jealous of Burnside
And sent him a harsh and icy order.
Take the bridge and cross immediately,
Or relinquish your command to another.

A mass of bodies blocked the crossing.
Bloated dead bobbed in filthy water.
Finally, brave New Yorkers stormed across
And concluded the horrible slaughter.

The Rebs retreated to a wooded ridge
Several hundred yards above the creek.
Suddenly our men we were cut off and trapped,
No way to advance or retreat.

Unable to retreat, their sharpshooters were
Abandoned high in the trees to die.
Refusing to come down or surrender,
We shot them down like birds in the sky.

We could not move forward to fight our foe.

We were trapped in a hopeless situation.
Men were starved, thirsty, and exhausted.
We needed a miraculous solution.

Sergeant McKinley came forward to see
If he could provide us with some relief.
Perhaps he could bring us some provisions,
Maybe a cool drink or something to eat.

Seeing our plight, he returned to the rear,
Began loading a wagon and hitching a team.
He returned toward our position.
Loaded with water, meat, coffee and beans.

On his way forward with our provisions,
Twice he was stopped by military staff.
If you pass, you will certainly be killed.
There is organized resistance in your path.

Seeing our circumstance was precarious,
He concluded he would make a desperate dash.
He whipped his team into frenzy
And bolted from the woods with a crash.

Rebel soldiers could see the oncoming team
And opened with rifle fire and cannon.
Their fusillade was so intense
It ripped off the back of the wagon.

With his team all sweaty and lathered
Reaching safety, he and a volunteer
Were met by grateful officers and men
Who gave him a thankful cheer.

Our men were exhausted and famished.
Soldiers pushed forward in groups of ten.
McKinley served the rations; it was
An act of mercy as he fed the men.

A critically wounded man was loaded
On the wagon and spoke through his bandage.
"God bless the lad; he has saved my life.
On the field, I've never seen such courage."

I heard Mr. Hall tell this vignette
Of Jackson saving Sergeant McKinley.
While it was a good story much later,
I cannot speak for its veracity.

Observing all this from a quarter mile
Were Stonewall Jackson and a sharpshooter
I'm able to kill him from this distance.
We will draw no fire. There is no danger.

Stonewall said *I have watched him today*
And he has courage. Put down your weapon.
Something tells me that he will go far, as
Stonewall rode off sucking on a lemon.

McClellan declined to give us fresh troops.
As a result, we were forced to yield
The hard won, bloody ground to AP Hill.
One charge from us could have secured the field.

That night we heard the pitiful wounded
Crying for help and aid from the meadow.
We prepared to fight our enemy.
Certainly victory would come tomorrow.

At Burnside's Bridge the dead and mangled men
Were strewn all over the battle site.
Surgeons were soon working on the wounded.
The smell of chloroform filled the night.

The battle did not resume the next day.
Rumors were new troops were reinforcing Lee.
McClellan said he needed more soldiers
Before he could engage Lee's Army.

Two days later Lee withdrew from Sharpsberg.
We had given up an important chance.
Our men were depressed and embittered.
And unrest circulated in our ranks.

With Lee escaped to Virginia,
We sent fifteen men to canvass the field
To retrieve any useful equipment for us

And see what spoils Antietam might yield.

All the men saw was the wreckage of war:
Stacks of body parts and men stripped bare,
The terrible stench of dead animals
Floated over, permeating the air.

After Antietam—Fall 1862

Our unit was relieved from combat action
To positions that offered safety.
We camped on the Potomac River
A short distance from Harper's Ferry.

In the early fall, President Lincoln
Reviewed the battle of South Mountain
With generals McClellan and Burnside
Who accompanied him to Antietam.

At Harper's Ferry, he reviewed us.
He seemed deeply sad as he went by,
Weighed down by the horrors of war
Refusing to look our men in the eye.

Depressing shadows crossed his face when
They gave him our flag with its bullet holes.
He met our eyes with grief and agony,
Forever searing a mark on our souls.

We set up camp at Fort Maskell
Where we would spend the oncoming winter.
It was a suitable place for our men
By the Falls of the Kanawha River.

McKinley was furloughed to Ohio
To recruit and fill open positions.
Told if he brought nine enlisted men,
He would get a lieutenant's commission.

He returned early to Camp Maskell,
In the closing days of 1862.
The commissioned Second Lieutenant

Adjusted quickly to his new duty.

Respectively recorded,
A Fellow Soldier

✶ ✶ ✶ ✶

Lt. McKinley
The newly commissioned Lt. McKinley returned to his unit after a winter break and later showed courage at the battle of Winchester.

THEODORE ROOSEVELT
President 1901-1909

Robert Introduces the Theodore Roosevelt Poems

The sudden death of William McKinley
Brought Roosevelt to the Presidency,
And he moved quickly to transition
And establish his administration.
He was a whirlwind of energy,
Moving to relieve our anxiety.
He let us know he would be retaining
Cabinet appointees, staff, and employees.
His announcement was well received,
And I make no pretense; I was relieved.
He was our President at forty-three,

At the very young age of twenty-three,
He had been elected to the New York
Assembly, then tried ranching in Dakota.
He traveled to the Yellowstone in Montana
And danced with the Hopi in Arizona.

Then he returned to New York City,
Distinguishing himself with contributions
To the US Civil Service Commission.
He was selected as head of the Police Board.
Respected as a tough, honest leader,
He received an appointment to be
Assistant Secretary of the Navy.
When the US declared war with Spain,

Roosevelt resigned to lead the Rough
Riders. He became famous for leading
A charge at San Juan Hill in Cuba.
After the war, he ran for Governor
Of New York and was easily elected.
Because of his national popularity,
McKinley picked him to be his Vice
Presidential running mate in 1900.
No administration had ever taken
Such a hold upon the imagination
Of the American public as that
Of Theodore Roosevelt's family.

His children were all over the Mansion.
Their pony became part of the scene.
In time, it seemed normal to see
The pony on the second floor
Or taking a ride on the elevator.
The children rode bicycles and roller
Skated on the polished hard wood
Floors. No bed was too expensive
Nor chair too elegantly upholstered
To be excluded as a resting place
For pets. No fountain was too deep
For a dip. Each child had a pair of stilts
For playing tag or climbing stairs.

At times, he constructed physical tests
For his ministers to see if they could last
And survive hard hikes, and if they passed
They found their access much improved.
Rumors circulated that he approved
Promotions based how a person hiked.

Once, I was told to take him a message
While he was hiking below the bridge.
He asked me to hike, and that led to
Scheduled outings. Arduous hikes
Granted me access and advantages.

Tonight, I will read ten poems, which I put
In Grant's old leather box years ago.

JOHN KERR

What follows are sonnets, reflections, an ode,
Insights on living the strenuous life
Which was his guiding philosophy.

★ ★ ★ ★

A Clash of Egos
Teddy Roosevelt enjoyed making John Singer Sargent uncomfortable whenever Sargent attempted to paint Roosevelt's portrait. After several futile attempts, Sargent caught Roosevelt on the stairs and painted his portrait. This painting is companion to side-by-side letter poems by Sargent and Roosevelt, which describe each man's view of the other.

Two Strong Wills

John Singer Sargent was a talented
Portrait artist but known to be a strong
Willed, somewhat difficult task master
When he had important clients sitting
For him. He was not ready for the will
Of the President who took great delight
In irritating Mr. Sargent at
Every opportunity. It took many
Meetings for them to agree on the
Place where the Presidential portrait would
Be painted. Mr. Sargent followed
On the President's heels from room to room
Arguing that it was long overdue
For the painting to start. As Mr.
Roosevelt bolted up the main staircase,
He turned to shout at his pursuer.

When he stopped on the landing, Sargent
Shouted that was the site where he would paint.
Roosevelt agreed but continued
His torment of the artist by standing
For only a half hour each afternoon.
It was a wonder to all the household
That the portrait was ever completed.

I found the two poems in a file
When the Roosevelts departed.
Both Sargent and Roosevelt enjoyed
The tug of war of wills and the result.

* * * *

John Singer Sargent painted Theodore Roosevelt's Portrait—1903

Dear Friend

I

When I began the President's portrait,
(And it was against my better judgment)
He had no concept of still or quiet.
He could not pose for more than a minute

II

I insisted on the staircase landing
As the portrait site. Under constant stress,
Even to my suggestion of clothing,
He objected to wearing formal dress.

III

In my presence, he was irritated.
Posing like a wounded pugilist
He did his best to make me feel wretched.
His grip turned the stair rail to sawdust.

IV

I was restricted to one half hour
Of sitting each day, as if an artist
Works as a mere cartoon illustrator
Transferring images to oiled canvass.

V

I had labored on this one yearlong.
It will be seen at a future banquet.
I have now come to see that I was wrong.
With no doubt, this is my finest portrait.

Sargent

Dear Son Kermit

I

I was made to sit for a new portrait,
(And it was against my better judgment)
To sit for hours with Singer Sargent
And smell his canvass, brushes and pigment.

II

I decided that the staircase landing
Would be the best place to paint my picture.
At least I stopped his endless talking,
But I refused to dress like a waiter.

III

My pose showed me thoroughly modern
Firmly, my hand grasped the balustrade
Showing I was strong and fit to govern
As I led the American parade.

IV

To pass the time, I asked him questions
His short answers showed him to be shallow.
He could not carry a conversation
On our Hemisphere's debt to Monroe.

V

But it happened as if by magic,
During the year, to the paint and pigment.
Blank canvass became artistic classic.
With no doubt, this is my finest portrait.

Father

The President Suggested a Reading Program

The family enjoyed quiet evenings,
Spending their time playing cards and reading
At home. From the oldest to the youngest
Each always had a book or magazine
In his hand. The President could consume
As many as three books in a sitting.
The President was well read, and authors
Were invited to read from their works.
A steady stream of important writers
Called at the White House. I asked Mr.
Cortelyou if he would speak with the President
And obtain his recommendations for
A reading program to be a part of
My self-improvement exercises.

In due time, the President sent me his
Thoughts. They were unvarnished in his likes
And dislikes of authors and their works.
Looking back over the years, his guidance
Was impeccable and stood the test of
Time. He did not care for Mark Twain, called
Him a Prized Idiot, but he liked
His work. E. A. Robinson was one of
His favorites, and he supported him
Financially. Henry James called on
Several occasions. I could not read
His books, but I liked Robert Browning's
Magnum opus, *The Ring and the Book.*

The President gave me the wonderful
Gift of guidance and support. He led me
Down the path of knowledge and enjoyment.

* * * *

A Letter to My Young Friend

Word has reached me though our mutual friend
Your request that I might possibly send
Some suggestions of books you should read.

Because you have the desire to succeed,
With a commitment to better yourself,
The best place to start is at my bookshelf.

Before I begin, some words of caution.
The list differs for every person.
It all becomes a matter of preference
The favorites you hold in reverence.
The works that you ultimately embrace
Are selected as a matter of taste.

Weight of personal taste in reading
Is as important to me as eating.
I like oranges, peaches, pears and apples.
I have no taste for prunes and bananas.
My tastes vary when evaluating Shakespeare.
I enjoy *Macbeth* and despise King Lear
Even though I am told that the latter
Should be ranked as high as the former.
As you can see, I have some favorites.
I adore Othello but not Hamlet.

Fond of the classics, a man or woman
Will seek works their minds and souls demand.
Persons who think reading a drudgery
Are doomed to dwell in their mind's debris.
I offer no relief to a person
Who has such little imagination.

All that said, let me begin to outline
Some authors that fit my reading guideline.
I will construct a personal template
Of topics, titles and authors to submit
As suggestions that develop and strengthen
The effort to expand your education.
Robert Louis Stevenson's *Treasure Island*
Will get you started and is regarded
Highly. When done and ready to talk
About it, see me and we'll go for a walk.

From there take on *Tom Sawyer* and *Huck Finn*,
Books by one of my favorites, Mark Twain.

Twain is one of America's best authors;
At some level our most able philosopher.

Advance to Keats's *Ode on a Grecian Urn*
Then come by and tell me what you learned.
Read Edgar Poe's *To Helen* for glimpses
Into the mind of creative genius.

Read books on adventuring and hunting.
See Africa through books on exploring.
Remember important historians
Such as Macauley, Parkman and Gibbon.
You will revere history and admire
The Rise and Fall of the Roman Empire.

Our Declaration of Independence
Illuminates our founders' brilliance.
And read our nation's effort to restore
The Union in Ulysses Grant's *Memoirs.*

You are now ready to read epic poetry.
So try your skill with Whitman and Dante.
Both wrote in the language of the marketplace.
You gain much by reading *Leaves of Grass.*
I treasure the poems of Robert Browning.
His *Flight of the Duchess* is inspiring.
Try to read all the poems of Tennyson.
You will find nourishment in *In Memoriam.*

Sample the works of Irving Hawthorne,
Shelly, Gray, Longfellow and Emerson.
With Goethe, Scott, Cooper, Bierce and Dickens,
You will make friends with heroes and villains.

To read the best of contemporary skill
Try E. A. Robinson's *The House on the Hill.*
I got him appointments that let him write,
And he gave us *The Children of the Night.*

I think these ideas will be a good start
To challenge your brain and open your heart.
Later, we will move on to the best

Literature and attempt to digest
Immanuel Kant's mind-bending Second
Treatise on Human Understanding.
We will examine the human condition
Reading *Paradise Lost* by John Milton.

Young friend, this is my suggested list.
However, I think I would be remiss
To not give a list of authors I find
Almost useless for a thoughtful mind.

I have nothing but contempt and disdain
For that miserable snob Henry James
As well as weak Henry David Thoreau
And the base, immoral Emil Zola.

A novel I loathe is *The Octopus*,
Written by the charlatan Frank Norris.
I have mixed feelings about Tolstoy.
Some of his works are good. Others annoy
Me. *Dishonesty* about class despair
Is the best effort of Upton Sinclair.
So these are my first recommendations
On which you can build your reading foundation.
Finally, young friend, I want to convey
My best wishes for your reading journey.

* * * *

Jefferson Davis Wrote to President Roosevelt

The terrible war between the Union
And the Confederacy destroyed
The South but preserved our national
Unity. President Roosevelt made
It clear that he had great respect for the
Officers and gentlemen who led the
Southern Army during the terrible war.

He had utter disdain and contempt for
The political leaders of the South
Who drove the South into the fire of war,

Destroyed their way of life and brought
Upon them the pestilence and woe
Of a defeated people for their own
Oily, venal political purposes.

The President asked me to edit his
Ballade response to Jefferson Davis
Prior to sending it. I made no changes
To it, but I transcribed a copy.

* * * *

An Open Letter to Jefferson Davis

My dear sir: Recently you have written
Asking that I not call you a traitor.
What else should one call your acts of treason
That sent tens of thousands of our youngsters
By your hand into senseless slaughter.
Yours and Benedict Arnold's treachery
Are a disgrace to our nation's honor.
God bless this great Union and keep us free.

For private gain, you stoked secession.
With all the moral conscience of an adder,
You infected people with your poison.
Then you write that galling letter
Which I read and tossed in the gutter.
Sir, you have no concept of loyalty—
Better you roam and live as a beggar.
God bless this great Union and keep us free.

The nerve you show to ask for a pardon.
You could have ended the war much sooner.
You should have spent your life in a dungeon
Because of the hardships our prisoners
Faced in your hellholes after capture.
You extended the war asking spent Lee
To send your young boys into war's shredder.
God bless this great Union and keep us free.

Jefferson Davis, please cease your clamor,
For you, sir, are our nation's enemy.
Listen closely to my heartfelt prayer:
God bless this great Union and keep us free.

* * * *

Money, an Inner Conflict

The president was not a wealthy man.
He worried if he would have sufficient
Savings to support his family when
He left office and returned to the
Life of an ex-president and former
World leader. He had helped to resolve

Hostilities between Japan and its
Rival Russia. For his work, he won the
Nobel Prize for peace, and with it, a cash
Award of forty thousand dollars, which
Accompanied the honor of the prize.

He felt inner conflict regarding
Money. He enjoyed the prestige
Of winning the Peace Prize, but he felt he
Would be subject to wide criticism
If he accepted money for doing
His job as President of the country.

* * * *

Roosevelt and his family in 1903

Thinking About the Nobel Prize

The word here is that I will win the prize
And with it some forty thousand dollars.
Rumor has it that is about the size
Of the financial portion of the honors.

I do not want to do anything foolish,
But I am troubled by a question.
Would it appear as naively quixotic
To reject this most generous stipend?

Money should not be paid for making peace
Treaties between belligerent nations.
It was my duty to arrange a cease
Fire and then have them lay down their weapons.

This would be like a fireman rescuing
Someone, or heroic acts in battle,
Or a man saving someone from drowning
Receiving cash in lieu of a medal.

I conclude there is no alternative
But give the grant to some public purpose.
I will ask my family to forgive
Me. As President, I must be cautious.

* * * *

Col. Theodore Roosevelt and the Rough Riders

Theodore Roosevelt and His Rough Riders

During the preparations for war with
Spain, Roosevelt resigned his job as
Assistant Secretary of Navy
And helped form a cavalry with men
Who were skilled horsemen. He recruited
Cowmen from the West and polo players
From the East. These men fought at San Juan Hill
In Cuba. They were called Rough Riders.

They became celebrated throughout
America and widely respected.
The President remained in contact
With his ex-Rough Riders for many years.

Long after he left the White House, during
President Wilson's term in the middle
Of the Great War in Europe, he asked
For permission to raise another force
Of Rough Riders to help fight the Germans
In France. He said it would be an honor
For him to die in battle leading the
Rough Riders. President Wilson, who did
Not care for all the personal attacks
He had received from Roosevelt, sent
Him a reply, stating if Roosevelt
Would guarantee that he would die fighting,
Then he might consider the proposal.

Ode to the Rough Riders

We recruited hardy men from the Plains.
We looked for accomplished horsemen
Who had saddle skills and touch with the reins.
Our objective was to transform cowmen
Into cavalry. We required drills
With rifles. They became deadly marksmen.
It took men of great courage and strong will
To hear the charging call of the bugler
And struggle to the crest of San Juan Hill.

Amidst the hell of the enemy's fire,
We captured munitions and banners.
Our brave men showed courage and valor.
Far from their homes, these courageous ranchers
Became known as America's Rough Riders.

* * * *

Living at the Edge

His commitment to physical fitness
And mental toughness was his life time goal.
He practiced strenuous exercise
And insisted that all persons around
Him engage in physically active
Programs. He said that individuals
And nations must live in constant training.

He believed that the strenuous life
Was necessary for advancement
Of America's national purpose.
During his administration we saw
An almost endless parade of trainers,
Wrestlers, tennis champions, horsemen, coaches
And boxers. He enjoyed riding with the
Family, and when no one could go with
Him, he would invite me along for a
Spirited gallop on the nearby trails.

I witnessed broad sword battles between
General Wood and him. He enjoyed
Games of medicine ball with members of
His cabinet and took poorly trained
Members of the military on long hikes.

He outlined his doctrine of the life
Of activity in a speech before
He became President. The two poems that
Follow were written many years apart.
The first one was left behind when he left
The White House. The second one was given
To me not long before the President died.

Live the Strenuous Life

Live the doctrine of the strenuous life.
Live not the doctrine of ignoble ease.
Evade not, nor turn from the noble strife.
Consider sloth a dishonorable disease.

The nobler man does not shrink from danger,
Engaged with vigor in life's contest,
He finds his purpose in productive leisure
And achieves the highest form of success.

A man freed from economic turmoil,
Because he worked earlier with good purpose,
Should perform some nonremunerative toil
In the arts, letters, research or science.

Mindful of the life of aspiration,
We should castigate the idle wealthy.
For individuals and the nation
Striving after higher things is healthy.

Providing a Square Deal for our people
Based on thrift and business energy,
Built with American brains and muscle
Grants us material prosperity.

In world affairs, we must show strength of heart.
With a clear vision beyond our borders,
Standing our ground is the important part,
Never forced to kneel before others.

Now the torch has passed. It is our turn
To accept the task and heed the call.
And woe to us if we fail to govern.
The Union preserved will surely fall.

✷✷✷✷

Consequences of the Strenuous Life
(Vigor di Vita)

Years have passed since I spoke those lines.
I see them from a perspective of time.
First thoughts of these came when as a mere boy
I lived a difficult life with scant joy:
Frail, asthmatic, and very weak
With eye problems and unable to speak
Clearly. It came to me that I could be
Master of my physical destiny.

Commitment to an athletic program
Set me on the endless path to overcome
Limitations of my physical body
And increase my mental energy.
I created a new being over time.
I became Mary Shelly's Frankenstein,
Except this one excelled in debate
And spoke on *Limits of the Modern State*.

To be aggressive, I learned boxing.
To increase strength and agility, wrestling
Proved essential. That led to tramping
In the Adirondacks and rough camping
In the Catskills, most useful for ranching
In the Dakotas which are unforgiving
Like the Amazon Basin while rafting.
In Africa, I enjoyed hunting.
On the Mississippi, I tried boating.
Back in New York, I kept up my rowing.
Though in retrospect, it sounds frenetic,
I mixed politics with athletics.
I was much like the actor who turned
Into the stage character he played.

The cost of my adventuring has been high.
While sparring with my coach, I lost an eye.
And in the basin of the Amazon,
In dangerous, splendid isolation
I contracted an unknown infection
Which could kill me or cost an election.

Former President Roosevelt Toured the West

Above all else, the President was curious.
He was well read on a wide variety
Of subjects. Animals fascinated
Him, and he was an authority on
Birds. After he left the Presidency,
He took an extended trip to Europe
And Africa. On his return, he could
Not hide his disappointment and contempt
For the manner in which his successor
William Howard Taft was not following
Roosevelt's plans for how the country should
Be run. He decided to take a trip
Out West to get away from politics
For a period of time. From the West,
He sent back several observations
On landscapes, animals, and a special
Visit to see the Hopi Snake Dance
Ceremony, which was held at
Third Mesa in Arizona.

His descriptions of the birds in Yellowstone
And the vivid Arizona sunsets
Show his remarkable insights to the
Natural beauty that surrounds our lives.
Much later after the Tafts left office,
Mr. Ike Hoover gave me these writings.

* * * *

The Ousel

A miracle of nature is music
Made for man's enjoyment and sung by birds.
Their daily rituals bring intrinsic
Joy to all. Their songs and signals are heard
From dawn to dusk. The song of the Ousel
Is a favorite of mine. His melody
Reaches a symphonic range, and this trill
Is provided to the world cheerfully.

I have heard them sing while perched by a stream
In the sanctuary of Yellowstone Park.
I much prefer to hear the Ousel sing
Than the Solitaire or the Meadowlark.

Our songbirds need thoughtful conservation.
We commit ourselves to their preservation.

* * * *

The Hopi Snake Dance

While in the West, I was in Hopi land
Enjoying the customs and culture firsthand.
I asked if there was any chance
To see the famous Hopi Snake Dance.
As a former great chief of the nation,
They extended me an invitation.

The Snake Dance is a yearly prayer for rain
That enables the Hopis to sustain
Their way of life. Downpours are female.
The thunderstorm with lightning is the male.

There are two parts to the ceremony:
One is private, held in secrecy.
The first is held in a room or Kiva
Where priests cleanse the snakes for the drama.
Inside a Kiva, I sat on the floor,
About four feet from the sacred altar.
Against the wall lay thirty-odd rattlesnakes,
All of whom looked wide awake.

Several ribbon snakes were in a pot,
Being too lively to remain uncaught.
Sitting on the floor were several priests
Who from time to time gently released
Snakes from a woven straw basket
Onto the outer edge of a blanket.

The snakes remained calm with no distress
And were kept together near the dais.
Painted on the floor of the Kiva a picture
Of a coyote circled by four rattlers
Was hemmed on three sides by lightning sticks
Standing upright in little clay relics.
The lightning stick is strong medicine
To be used by the tribal chieftain.
On the fourth side were erect eagle plumes
Needed for the ceremony, I assumed.
The snakes close behind me never rattled
Or indicated stress or signaled
A hostile sign of malice or rancor.
They appeared to be without anger.
As one glided sinuously astray
Toward me, a priest turned it away
By stroking its head with a large eagle
Feather and gently turning the reptile.

When the ceremony began, at least
Eighty snakes were controlled by ten priests,
Half of them rattlers, some bulls, and ribbons
At the feet of the deputy chieftains.
Moves in the room were made without hurry
And gave the feel of no need to worry.

The leader began by puffing some smoke
At a small bowl and chanting to invoke
The spirits with a pinch of sacred meal.
Other priests joined his prayerful appeal
Uttering a single word like amen
With words said over and over again.

In the half light, it became a strange scene,
And the priest's faces grew serene.
When the volume of the chanting grew sharply,
Its content gained in intensity.

Two men stooped over and began to take
Some of the larger more venomous snakes
To priests stationed at the washbowl stand
Who grasped four or five snakes in each hand.

Chanting accelerated its rhythm
Until it reached a vocal spasm.
Suddenly the chanting rose to a scream.
It was if I were in an eerie dream.

Snakes were thrust into the bowl of water,
Tangling snakes and hands in the chamber.
Immediately, the snakes were withdrawn,
And from a distance of fifteen feet, thrown
Across the room against the altar
Knocking thunder sticks to the floor.

After the snakes were bathed in water,
They were herded back with eagle feathers.
Chants were renewed, but they grew softer.
Sacred meal was scattered; it was over.

The dance began that afternoon at five,
And as the dancers began to arrive
The snake priests wore kilts with fringed leather
And a headdress with an eagle feather.

Fox skin girdles in the afternoon light
Contrasted with their bodies painted white.
They danced on a slab as they twirled,
Cajoling and singing to the Underworld.
Young girls rested, near a large stone pillar,
With sacred meal to ensure good weather.
Then as couples, the men made their entrance.
One had a snake in his mouth as they danced.

One of each couple was the snake bearer.
His partner kept the snake calm with a feather,
Stroking the ace-of-spades shaped head
Of the snake as the dance procession led
The dancing line moving in wide circles,
Until the couples held all the reptiles.

At last, each man carried a bundle
Of snakes in his mouth, being most careful
When he exchanged the snakes and then place
New rattlers with heads free near his face.

And as we neared the end of the day
All the snakes were carried this way.
Snakes were thrown at the base of the pillar.
Ending the dance, we heard distant thunder.

With a yell, men scooped up the reptiles
And ran from the plaza at all angles.
Some went north and west over a cliff's edge.
Others went south and east, jumping a ledge.

The snakes were abandoned out on the plain
Or the cliff, never to be seen again.
We watched the return of the runners
Who were cleansed in Medicine Water.

I returned to my camp exhausted,
Knowing that I had seen something sacred,
And though I was emotionally spent,
I returned from this ritual event
With a deep and sincere admiration
For this pageant of ancient devotion.

Later that evening I sat in wonder.
In the distance, we heard rolling thunder.

* * * *

Navaho Sunset

Hiking in the land of the Navaho,
We entered a mystical canyon.
Framed on the rim above, a rainbow
Welcomed us to splendid isolation.
Late afternoon colors began dancing
On the canyon walls: ochre and amber
Reflected in the water from the spring.
Soft colors faded into burnt umber.
Our evening sky turned from blue to purple
Weaving a blanket of vermillion

With stripes and layers of warm, subtle
Hues spiced with saffron and melon.
Nature provides an exquisite beauty
In this golden, salmon shaded country.

* * * *

WILLIAM HOWARD TAFT
President 1909-1913

Getting the call from Roosevelt that the Republican Party had nominated Taft.

Robert Introduces the Taft Poems

When President Roosevelt's term ended,
The house staff felt a deep sense of relief.
The whirlwind of his administration
Was replaced by a more peaceful cadence.
The Roosevelts were raucous and vocal.
Quickly, Mrs. Taft involved herself

In every aspect of household affairs.
She took control of all entertainment
And inspected the guest invitation lists
Thoroughly. Nonfavorites of hers often were
Excluded from guest lists at State dinners.
She relished being First Lady.

Someone has described the Roosevelt
Administration as one nonending
Fourth of July celebration.
The Taft administration was more like
The long day after the Fourth of July.

As we continue to empty the old
Leather box, I have selected seven
Poems from different times in Taft's adult
Life. The last one was written when he was
Finally named Chief Justice of the
Supreme Court, the position he always
Coveted, more than the Presidency.

I have included poetic exchanges
Between Taft and Root when as Governor
Of the Philippines, Taft was charged with
The Pacification of islands
Obtained in the Spanish American War.

Taft's wife and President Roosevelt were
In favor of his ascending to the
Presidency. A late night exchange in
The White House library may shed light on
Their ambitions for Taft's political
Future and his place in our History.

* * * *

After Dinner in the Library—1906

Thank you for serving sandwiches and sweets
To me this afternoon. These special treats
Are after dinner evening favorites
Of mine and served late after banquets.

Assuredly, I am agreeable
To inform you of last evening's mirthful
Conversation in the upper library
Which was used to ensure privacy.

As Mrs. Taft and the Secretary
Were escorted into the library,
The President sat Mr. Taft away
From the sofa and next to the sweet tray.
Mrs. Taft agreed to act as hostess
And manage the tea and coffee service.

I was on Personal Servant duty,
Responsible for keeping coffee
In the silver pot and replenishing
Tasty snacks and sweets during the evening.

I was to stand outside the open door
And enter only to replenish food before
A tray or cup or plate was empty.
I was the gastronomic sentry!

So you find that intriguing? Please draw near,
And I will tell you how it went from there.
Three agendas were in the room that day.
Each one of the three had a part to play
In this complex political drama,
To be painted in a future diorama.

The pleasures of golf
President and Mrs. Taft enjoy a game of golf in the early morning.
Although Taft was a large man with an unorthodox swing, he enjoyed the game.
The poem of the same name is in the collected poems.

After a brief pause in conversation,
The President said that continuation
Of his work in administrations
Following his term required that intentions
Be signaled, and he had selected
The man he hope would be elected.

Then he spoke in a booming voice
Like an actor in a romantic farce,
That he was a powerful Swami
Possessing the power of prophesy.

Both Tafts were completely astounded.
I could not speak, struck dumfounded.
Our host seeing complete consternation
Pressed forward with this exclamation.
*As seventh son of a seventh daughter
I possess and use clairvoyant power.
I see a man close to the White House grounds,
Weighing over three hundred fifty pounds.
The air imparts a sense of dread,
For something heavy hangs over his head.*

The Tafts recovered and tried to smile,
But they looked as if they were on trial.

*I am unable to see through the haze
And identify the weight with my gaze.
The Vision becomes focused clearly.
Now it looks like the Presidency.*

On hearing these words, Mrs. Taft laughed.
She became more visibly relaxed.

*In a cloud, the Vision disappears.
We need to see if it returns and clears.
Suddenly the Vision returns and shifts.
Hanging aloft is the Chief Justiceship
Of the Supreme Court. Do I have the right
As Swami to decide Taft's fate tonight?*

Turning to Mrs. Taft, he asked
Her wish. Without hesitation she gasped.

*Please make it the Presidency if you can.
The graveyard of the Court is not my plan.*

Then the Swami asked for direction
And guidance for Mr. Taft's selection.

*As for this grave matter, there is no question.
Being Chief Justice is my salvation.*

Reflecting, the Tafts sat for a moment
While the President remained silent.
In unison, all three began laughing.
I reentered and began filling
Empty coffee cups. When I completed
My tasks, the President then relieved
Me of further work and said I was free
To return to my kitchen duty.

The President's decision will be made
Soon. One thing is certain; he will not fade
Into travel and books. He is too young.
He will not slow down until he has wrung
Commitments to follow his policies
And continue to build his legacy.

It is essential that you keep this secret,
And remind your friends to be most discreet.
Disclosure would cost me my job and lessen
My access to valuable information.

I owe your friends much and ask they respect
My situation. Now as I exit
Let me thank you for the new position
And opportunity for advancement.

* * * *

Governor of the Philippines

Early in his public service, Taft went
To the Philippines as the governor
In charge of exerting America's
Control of the Islands acquired as
A result of our successful war with
Spain. A series of cablegrams between
Taft and Elihu Root became grist in
The political campaign when Taft
Entered the presidential arena.

He was known to consume great amounts
Of food, and the combination of good chefs
And hot weather added extra pounds to the
Vastly overweight Governor Taft.

★★★★

In the Philippines

*To: William Howard Taft, Philippines Governor
From: War Secretary Root, Your Superior
Sir: Please send me forthwith a reasonable
Assessment of your work as soon as feasible.*

*To: War Secretary Root, My Superior
From: William Howard Taft, Philippines Governor*

Sir, please find below my professional
Assessments and some that are personal.

Professional Reflections

We are making progress, but it is slow.
Recent storms caused devastating setbacks
In planting schedules, so we must forego
Long term farming goals and react
To the potential of mass starvation
Among the people of the coastal plain
If we do not begin cultivation
Soon in humid weather and gentle rain.

Personal Reflections

We live in Malacañang Palace.
With high walls, it is suited for sleeping.
It is not far from Government offices.
This tropical climate requires eating
Often to maintain vital forces
Of life. We are fortunate to have good
Cooks who prepare elaborate courses
And ample amounts of excellent food.

To maintain mental fitness and steadfast
Work schedules, I arise at first daylight
And start my day with a hearty breakfast
Mandated by a healthy appetite.

At breakfast, I receive excellent quality
Coffee, juices, toast, butter and mangoes
Served in acceptable quantities
With marmalade, bacon, eggs and oranges.
The temperature may reach ninety degrees
Shortly after I have concluded brunch.
At one thirty, my physician agrees
My best regimen is a robust lunch.

At lunch, we eat crabs, lobsters and beefsteaks
With shrimp, cheese, salad, fruit and strawberry
Fritters. Jam accompanies griddle cakes
With butter, raspberries and honey.

One's vital life forces are drawn upon
By work, so we serve fruit, coffee cake
With almonds and dates in the late afternoon
Which has added to my substantial weight.

Professional Reflections

In April, I traveled to the mountain
Town of Baguio, which meant the stables
Were required for our transportation.
It was arduous work for our horses.

I rode horseback twenty-five miles in heat
That was intense under a broiling sun
Up a steep mountain to five thousand feet.
I withstood the trip well. Have no concern.

Reports often sound pessimistic
From here. If you need my explanations
Or reasons for being optimistic,
Please respond. I will answer your questions.

To: William Howard Taft, Philippine Governor
From: War Secretary Root, Your Superior

Sir, your cable arrived in due course.
My only question is, how is the horse?

* * * *

A Long Relationship with Yale

Yale University had a profound
Influence on the young student Will Taft.
His father had entered the school in
Eighteen twenty nine. Young Will Taft began a
Long history with Yale when he came to
School. From his freshman year through the rest
Of his professional life, he came back
To Yale at critical junctures in his
Life. He considered Yale to be his
Place for inspiration and nourishment.

In this poem, ex-President Taft reflects
On his association with the school:
As a freshman, on being offered
The presidency of Yale and then his
Return as a law professor before
He was named Chief Justice of the Court.

He asked, "Are we pushed by random
Chance or guided by complex harmony?"
Ex-President, Chief Justice Taft sent the
Poem to me when he returned by train
From New Haven to become Chief Justice.

* * * *

Yale Lies Deep in My Bones

1913

Red, yellow, and brown leaves scamper across
The campus, caught up in random, swirling

Gusts of wind. They signal the coming loss
Of a year with their haphazard dancing.

Pleasant sound of harmonized singing
Mixes in gently with the evening breeze.
Wind, leaves and song meld as one, creating
A beautiful and complex symphony.

A scent of smoke from a wood fire settles
Over the campus providing a sense
Of peace. In the distance, evening chorales
Add to this stew of sensory incense.

Has random wind or secret melody
Guided my life? Did cosmic accident
Play a role or a sentient deity or sentiment
Lead my decisions and earthly movement.

Somewhere is there a mathematician
Who can explain Wind with a cosmic
Formula or express with an equation
The Divine as revealed through music?

As for Yale and me, it remains unknown
Whether Wind or guided Harmony
Brought me to Yale. It became my keystone:
A place of learning and sanctuary.

1829

Yale lies buried deep in my family's bones.
Alphonso Taft left the family's home,
Intending to enroll at Amherst College.
Arriving there, someone gave him the knowledge
Of a larger school in Connecticut,
And without pausing a minute,
Like Aaron who crossed to Canaan,
He began his long journey into New Haven.

On arrival, he decided to apply.
The school's annual expenses were high.
Expenses ran to one hundred ten dollars.

More money could lead to sinful pleasures.
Students lived and studied in austere
Surroundings. Following his freshman year
He walked back to his home in Vermont
To help his family bring in the crops.

To emphasize leadership qualities,
He founded Skull and Bones fraternity
With other students and campus leaders,
Which included a few leading scholars.

Often, we would listen to him extol
Yale. In all his days, it was in his soul.

Arriving, my first sensation was music
Providing the freshman class with rhythmic
Original harmonies and playful songs.
It would be a relationship lifelong
In duration. Studies, where others sailed
And eased through effortlessly, I plodded.

With my classmates, I was popular.
My father disapproved. A scholar
Should focus on his studies and bury
The cultic charms of personality.
Plodding, I was salutatorian
Of the class, a crowning benediction

For my work. My father's fraternity
With some hesitation selected me.

If it were wind that blew my father here,
I was sent by musical deities.

1899

My dear brother, your correspondence gives
Insight as to how back and forth our lives
Change with unexpected opportunities
Available to us in the nineties.
I understand that you are authorized
To find out if I am interested

In becoming the next President of Yale.
If I did, what a convoluted trail
It would have been. A powerful gust
Of capricious Wind yielded a large harvest.
Now, I have contemplated the question
Whether I should return to New Haven.

Thank you, but I must ask you to withdraw
My name. It is that the practice of law,
The courts, and a judgeship are my future.
I see these as my crowning endeavor.
One other reason why I must decline:
I do not hold the Nazarene divine.
Yale's Presidents have been men of Christian
Beliefs. I do not accept their doctrine.

1913–1921

I left the White House eight years ago
And arrived at the New Haven depot.
Yale had offered me the Kent Chair of Law.
Instead of a chair, I thought a sofa
Of law might be more appropriate
Given my increasing amount of weight.

Word comes to me that President Harding
Will inform me that he is offering
My name again for national service.
He will name me Supreme Court Chief Justice.

What returns me to Yale, a sanctuary
Of scholarship and complex harmony?
Am I part of a celestial dance,
Or pushed by the wind of random chance?

Smells from the wood fires and dancing leaves
Combined with a joyful melody weaves
Magic on our senses. We now prepare
For new work, breathing in the afternoon air.

* * * *

The Pleasures of Golf

Looking fresh in morning light, Chevy Chase
Golf course is an oasis as we pass
Through the entrance, motoring passed the gate,
Breathing in the smell of freshly cut grass.

Golf provides a pleasant escape for me.
On the links, I am able to focus
On the game as I hit from the first tee.
Here no one irksome waits outside my office.

I play golf with my aide Mr. Archie Butt
Who is gifted with niblicks and mashies.
With a Haskell gutty, he makes me putt
Out then marches away with our caddies.

Golf's rules and traditions appeal to me:
A game of honor and integrity.

****

Cherry Blossoms

Awakening to a pleasant morning,
Washington is covered in pink and white.
We are enjoying a wonderful spring
Season. Imagine our surprise and delight
To witness blossoms of the cherry trees

Planted last year as a gift to enliven
Our spirits. Nellie Taft thought cherry blossoms
Would help enhance the Capitol basin.
Japan gave us the trees with delicate
Blossoms to terminate long winter's gloom.
The pink flowers are nature's intricate
Architectural sketch of graceful blooms.
Lovely cherry trees are part of the plan
For long-term alliances with Japan.

****

Taft Came Under Attack

President Taft began with a disadvantage.
He had never been exposed to rough
And tumble of political office.
He was much too open and inclusive.
He surrounded himself with too many
Persons against the legislative
Change he thought important to the nation's
Interests. Acting less a president
And more like a thoughtful Supreme Justice,
He soon lost support of his own party
Leaders. His opponents and the yellow
Press turned on him with wrathful vengeance.

Eventually, President Roosevelt
Returned to the States from Africa
And Europe. He placed stories in the
Press, expressing displeasure in the way
His successor was handling affairs
Of state. Wounded, Taft acted badly.

He spent much of his remaining time as
President dealing with an increasing
Irritation and frustration as his
Presidency derailed in front of
His eyes. He was happy when he was on
Long train trips away from Washington,
At his Yale Club dinners or playing golf.

The convention in Chicago was the
Low point in his life. Roosevelt bolted the
Convention and formed the Bull Moose Party.
When Taft and Roosevelt split the voters
It brought Woodrow Wilson to the White House.

* * * *

Stop the Bull Moose

Sir, attempts by your people to subvert
Our rules and seat your rowdy forces

Will drag this convention into the dirt.
This smells of grease paint and spilt liquor.
You are behaving like an actor,
Whose stage role has concluded skillfully,
Leaping on stage to play to the rafters.
Stop the Bull Moose from destroying our party.

Sir, your thinly veiled plan to desert
The convention was hatched in sewers
Of the nation. Stop it, you must assert.
This act smells of day-old burnt cigars.
You are behaving like a gifted dancer
Who continues on without the orchestra.
Stop behaving like a jilted lover.
Stop the Bull Moose from destroying our party.

Sir, please listen to us. Open your heart.
Political soot and ash foul the air.
We implore you. Call off your men and divert
From party ruin. It is the only fair
Solution. You two were a matched pair
Of leaders. Conclude this disharmony.
Step forward. Embrace your former partner.
Stop the Bull Moose from destroying our party.
Theodore Roosevelt, dampen your anger.

Theodore Roosevelt, dampen your anger.
Without us, you lack viability.
Withdraw. Show respect, a sense of honor.
Stop the Bull Moose from destroying our party.

****

A Dream Realized

President Warren G. Harding named
Ex-President Taft as the Chief Justice
Of the Supreme Court, a position he
Had wanted all of his professional
Life. He invited me to attend the
Opening of the Court when he took charge.
I made these notes in the courtroom.
It was the happiest I have ever
Seen him. He headed the Bench finally.

* * * *

Court Is in Session—1922

Order has been called.
The seal is burnished.
Our floor is waxed.
The furniture is polished.

Flags sit in gold standards
Attorneys are prepared.
The briefs are before us.
The plaintiff seeks justice.
We hear the defendant
Requesting our judgment.
We have a full docket.
Our courtroom is quiet.
We adjust the benches.
The solicitor rises.
Court is in session.

* * * *

WOODROW WILSON
President 1913-1921

Robert Introduces the Wilson Poems

Woodrow Wilson guided the destiny
Of America for two terms in the
White House. It was a time of upheaval
Throughout the world. During Wilson's first term,
Germany invaded France and dragged
England into a Great War, which caused
Much debate over the role that we should
Play in resolving the conflict between
The parties. President Wilson took a
Cautious approach to entering the war.

He received loud, public abuse from his
Political enemies. Roosevelt
Was caustic in his criticism of
The President. We thought it was poor taste
For him to be so outspoken in his
Attacks. Mrs. Wilson died during the
First term which caused deep, painful sadness
To the President and his lovely daughters.

Some ten months after Mrs. Wilson was
Buried, the President began to court
Mrs. Edith Galt, and before long they
Were engaged and married at her small
Home in Washington. It took us a great

Deal of imagination and hard work
To create the appropriate wedding.

In his second term, Wilson led us to
War in Europe. The trenches were living
Hell for our men, and many died there.
While the war was proceeding, we were struck
By an influenza plague that killed
Over a half million of our people.

President Wilson was involved in the
Development of the League of Nations
And fought to have the Treaty of Versailles
Ratified by the Senate. He lost the
Struggle. While campaigning for the Treaty
In the Western States, he suffered a
Debilitating stroke, which hampered
Him until the end of his eight years.

Today, I bring a song, which was sung by
Returning soldiers at a reception.
I have included a sad poem on the
Plague of nineteen eighteen, war poems read to
Congress, and one from a Princeton teacher
Of mathematics who mentored me.
I have put aside love notes and letters
And bitter reflections on the Treaty.

* * * *

Wilson opens the season at Griffith Stadium, April 20, 1916.

An Election of Three Sides.
Roosevelt, Taft and Woodrow Wilson became living proof of Pythagoras'
Theorem. At an isosceles triangular desk in Wilson's office, the three men review
the results of the 1912 election. The sum of the results of Roosevelt and Taft
squared equaled the square of Wilson's votes. This painting is a companion
to The Garden of Mathematical Delights and the Election of 1912.

War Speeches to Congress

April 2, 1917

Our world must be safe for democracy.
A lasting peace must be firmly planted
On foundations of freedom and liberty
Fixed on a base completely tested.

We seek no payment or indemnity.
We are here to champion all nations.
We ask no financial compensation
For the bloodshed by America's sons.

Tonight I stand before you asking you
To lead a peaceful people into war
To defend and protect freedom's values.
God help us, for we can do no other.

November 11, 1918

Now a supreme moment in history has come.
The object of the war is attained.
The world's free men have set their hearts upon
Lasting peace which can be realized.

The great nations, which associated
Themselves to destroy peace can now unite,
Pursuing disinterested justice
For their people, given as a birthright.

We must replace the selfish interests
Of competitive, warring nation states
With capable settlements to harvest
Peace, while the entire world watches and waits.

* * * *

An Influenza Pandemic

It started in India and struck the
Trenches in Europe with such horrible
Impact that no medicine could stop it.
We had no means of prevention or cure
For the disease. It was beyond science.

It became such a nightmare that drastic
Methods were employed to curb and halt
The spread of the disease. In the
Large cities, public gatherings came to
A halt. Funeral services were held
For no more than twenty minutes. Public
Workers were required to wear protective
Masks. A coughing, lung foaming painful death
Could come within hours of the first symptoms.

Then the virus had a new mutation.
It vanished from our stricken nation.

* * *

The Forgotten Plague of 1918–1919

The war in Europe was a manmade curse
Claiming more than sixteen million lives.
Influenza followed with the worst
Plague in history with fifty million
Deaths caused by the world epidemic.
Created by viral mutation,
The disease evolved to pandemic
Proportions. Soon the deadly infection
Spread to Versailles and caught Woodrow Wilson.
It struck America with virulence
And proceeded to kill a half million
By withstanding all Western medical science.

This scourge we call influenza
Was replaced by national amnesia.

* * * *

We Are Marching Home

A Song of the Great War: Verses and Refrain

Tenor: We are on our way home.
War has come to an end.
The threat of death is gone.
Now broken hearts can mend.

All. Refrain: Marching home, marching home.
We are marching home.
Lass, kiss my cheek
Dad, shake my hand.
We are marching home.

Baritone: War is gone forever.
Peace bought at a dear price.
We crushed the Kaiser,
Freeing Germany's vise.

All. Refrain: Marching home, marching home.
We are marching home.
Mom, cook my lunch.
Sis, hug my neck
We are marching home.

Bass: Our mission was sacred,
Coming back victorious,
Ending evil's hatred,
Honors all glorious.

All. Refrain: Marching home, marching home.
We are marching home.
Brother, love me.
Banker, help me.
We are marching home.

* * * *

Victory Celebrations

When the horrible war in Europe
Ended, the entire nation held joyous
Celebrations. Parades, firework displays
And welcome home rallies were given in
Honor of the returning troops at the
White House. President and Mrs. Wilson
Gave victory parties and medals to soldiers
And sailors and their families. It was
A time of relief and thankful prayer.

At one of the White House festivities
I heard a chorus sing the previous
Song. I kept a copy and put it in
My leather box as a reminder of
That evening with the returning soldiers.

* * * *

The Garden of Mathematical Delights.

My Introduction to Mathematics

A Princeton mathematics professor
Came by one day. My job was to usher
Him into the President's office when
Meetings ended with visiting firemen.

The two meetings seemed to last forever.
I was praying that they might go faster.
All we could do was engage in small talk
And keep our eyes on the hands of the clock.

After the third time we heard the clock chime,
I apologized for wasting his time.
He smiled and said a curious thing:
He asked if perhaps Time were slowing.
Could it be that Time decelerated?
What would it be like to see it halted?

I told him that his questions were intriguing
And wondered if Time might be loafing.
He found humor in my feeble answer
And then suggested Time could move faster
If we could understand the mathematics
Underlying our universe's physics.
He continued to talk about time and space:
Perhaps we could be in more than one place.

I told him I knew little of numbers, and
I had looked for a way to expand
My education. He said in his carriage
Were books and texts to improve my knowledge.

Thus began a teacher-student program
That evolved into a curriculum
That began with basic arithmetic,
Moved through the laws of geometry,
Mastered joys of trigonometry,
Then through calculus at the speed of light
And pierced learning's veil with new insight.

Long after President Wilson was buried,
The professor left school and retired.
In our final correspondence, he sent
The garden poem as his final present.

The garden is a classic pastoral,
Placed in a setting that is peaceful
But located far from the world we know.
It is a place where great thinkers can go
To test mathematical interests
With shepherds and shepherdesses.

Once a prodigy from another place
Arrived there traveling through time and space.
She was told before she could be welcome,
She was required to prove a theorem
Of Pythagoras using Woodrow Wilson's
Success in the nineteen twelve election
As laboratory for her trial
Test of the squares of a right triangle.

The garden is an interesting place,
Hidden to us in its own special space.
With chairs at meals for teachers and solvers
And loud collections of shapes and numbers.
The professor moved when he retired,
Leaving no forwarding address. I tried
To find him in vain. Then it came to me,
He was in the garden where he should be.

* * * *

The Garden of Mathematical Delights And the Election of 1912. A Pastoral Poem

Late in the evening, well after midnight
In a garden of numeric delights
A young shepherdess rose and declared
That a prodigy would be transferred
Into their society where numbers
Work on problems with teachers and solvers
To help achieve mathematical advancement
In a setting that is lush and verdant.

Next morning at the admission portal
The shepherdess greeted the new arrival.

Welcome to the garden. We expected
Your arrival when we were informed
That you had completed processing.
You were observed with a guide walking
Toward the garden, along the river.
Did you find the river soothing? Boulders
Below the surface create small wavelets
That dance on the rushing water's surface
With a digital kaleidoscopic
Waterfall of subtle colors. Aspic,
Tangerine and lemon-lime can transform
Those who come here to work in a warm
Nurturing environment. Rosemary
Bushes, sage, thyme and juniper berry
Perfume the air, providing those chosen
An ideal home for a contribution.

Now if you do not mind, please follow me.
We will walk the path to that grove of trees
Partnered in the distance near the lake.
Those are ancient Sequoias. There we take
Our breakfast and plan our work for the day.
We wanted you present early today.

You can observe our society in place
And see how each uses his time and space.
As we enter and approach the buffet,
Please hold back, I have something to say.
I will tell you how we sit at breakfast,
And with that explanation you will grasp
The hierarchy and organization
Which guides our work in this complex garden.
We divide ourselves among log tables
Hewn from seventeenth century fables
Which ease complicated operations
Of large number calculations.
We see ourselves in bold reflections
On highly polished logarithms.

Tables are usually reserved
Until all participants have been served.
At the first table, the one with the best view,
Sit the teachers and solvers who renew
Each morning their discussion over
Impediments they encountered,
Which worked against their research interests
During the period between breakfasts.
I should pause at this point and bring
To your attention issues concerning
Travel to adjacent or distant spheres
And methods we use to control Time here.

Our shepherds and shepherdesses control
Time and space for themselves, using the bowl
Of this universe to ride a Helix Twine
To places and ages Albert Einstein
Gave us a ticket in Nineteen Fourteen.

As example, the journey from your
Previous dimension left you unsure
As to the distance you had traveled
Or the amount of time that transpired
As you made a passage to this dimension
And arrived at our space-time Station.

The answer depends on when you started
And exactly from where you departed,
All relative to where we were in space.
Did our Time moved forward or retrace?
You came not so far but very distant.
Millions of year miles were but an instant.

That said, let us resume our discussion
Of the members of our organization
And what transpires at our early meetings
Between tables of our diverse groupings.

Occupying the next table are numbers,
Including generally positive integers.
Some numbers see themselves as real.
Others make no pretense. They are unreal
In every sense. Numbers apparently rational
Metamorphous into irrational
Numbers without so much as a warning.
With numbers, it is all about vying
For chairs in notational position,
And they struggle in their competition
With one another. The one called prime
Informs us constantly of his sublime
Nature and among numbers his supreme
Position in mathematical schemes.

Table two is noisy. Imaginary
Numbers tug back and forth, then disagree
With naturals and fractions who confront
Complex numbers and attack exponents.
There is a perceived hierarchy here.
Transcendental numbers try not to sneer
Openly at lesser formed colleagues
Embroiled in arithmetic intrigues.

Arabic numerals wear exotic
Costumes and claim that they are the classic,
Correct numeric representation
As opposed to those from the Roman nation.
Last week we had to stop the ordinals'
Endless bickering with the cardinals.

Numbers returned early from surgery
Today are sent into recovery
To receive care and consideration
From a difficult operation,
Such as one that needed long division,
Or one requiring multiplication.
A special problem rests with the healers:
Who is responsible for remainders?

We should move on to the problem table.
Here I am certain you will be able
To see that we have separate sections
For two different species of problems.

The first are those that have been solved,
But we ask teachers to stay involved
To provide more elegant solutions
And reduce required operations.
Refinements to the prime number theorem,
Improved ways for pi's calculation,
New insights for probability theory,
And proof of e's irrationality
Are examples of how our group functions
For elegant proof reductions.

The second approach to problems involve
New techniques for old issues to solve
Classic questions such as infinity,
Area, time, space, and number theory,
Curved surfaces of four dimensions,
Cartography, length and navigations.

I sense that you have already grasped
We work on problems that are passed

Backward to us. We cannot send a change
Forward. Our charter keeps us constrained.

The fourth table consists of forms and shapes
Which provide contextual images
Of issues needing visualization
In stating a potential solution.

Honors accrue to shapes that are chosen.
Each form, substance or shape stays in motion
In a continuous competition
For a teacher's or solver's attention.

Here are stately Cubes and their cousins Squares
And Rectangles who lie flat in an area
Near Trapezoid and Rhomboid families.
Points and Line Segments assist in theories.
Radius, Diameter and Circles
Show their relationship to Curved Surfaces.
Much earlier today a cute angle
And an equilateral triangle
Made a pact of mutual affection
With sisters Poly and Tetra Hedron.
The Parabolas, Grecian beauties,
Work hard to show their practicality.

The table is littered with models,
New and used, and a constant babble
Begins early with debates that surround
The table with walls of fragrant sound.

The loudest table is our number five.
Occupants here must compete to survive.
They are a sophisticated collection
Of mathematical operations
Loosely associated but linked,
Some in danger of becoming extinct.

Each day teachers and solvers walk through
The garden to this table to preview
The systems and resources they will need
To ensure that their projects can succeed.

This process causes endless bickering
Between systems and noisy clamoring
For the teacher's consideration
In making an important selection.

Let me point out some of the physical
Attributes of this place and the table.
A hierarchy of roses grace Trellis
Codes which cover each side of the terrace.
Woven rugs on the floor have Egyptian
References to Babylonian
Advances in the methods of counting
And progress in the system of numbering.

On the walls hang Pi Casso portraits
Of famous geometric forms and shapes.
Some of the forms find his work disturbing,
His violation of rules, unnerving.

The awesome tables were built of hand sawn
Logs from cedars in Lebanon
The cedars lend pleasant aromatics
To aid the science of mathematics

Notice the fine carving on each table.
It is the Nautilus shell, a symbol
That best defines a favorite problem,
So they adopted it as their emblem.

In session, Arithmetic engages
With protégés and cohorts, then embraces
Trusted workers: Addition, Subtraction,
Then Multiplication and Division
While speaking at length with Involution
Then tumbling over to Evolution.
On the far end, mighty King Calculus
Holds court with a deferential chorus
Of sycophants and able followers,
Always in the company of solvers.
Announcements his court will give a clinic
Bring us our heaviest space-time traffic.

Orthogonal to this sits Geometry,
Calculus once called Plain and Homely.
He shortened it to Plain much later,
But the damage was done. Water
Was over the dam, and intense hatred
Rose up between them and never abated.

Geometry holds onto her offspring
Analytic and Differential, grandchildren
Of Euclid who purchased some prime space
Close to here so they could have their own place.

Across from her sits Trigonometry
Near established inequalities,
But some of his work has found accord
With angles, triangles, and sides ignored
Too long. Libraries now ask someone to sine
For analog charts. Then someone must cosine
For checkout of early texts on Astronomy
If they plan to use Trigonometry.

Wrapped in its own internal drama,
Sits the ancient totem of Algebra
Close enough to speak to Geometry
And influence her long-term destiny.
Algebra has a hard task. He manages
Symbols and numbers while he operates
Heavy machinery of complex Equations
Amid lawyers who represent Functions.

Scattered around the table are collections
Of useful mathematical engines.
Some are well defined, proved Theorems.
Others are straightforward Algorithms.
Every conceivable Definition
Is here and sits with haughty Axioms
Who enjoy the company of Postulates
Though they lack the precision of Constants.

It is a magical place of rainbows
Created by Numerical Ratios

Of colors unknown by the other place:
Just for us in this special space.

It is now time for an introduction
To your shepherd for continuation
Through this mathematical Eden.
He is well respected in the garden
As a shepherd who knows our etiquette,
When you should speak and when to be quiet.
He will explain to you why you are here
And construct a test in another sphere.
He will permit access to the Teachers
If your test is passed by the Solvers.

The shepherd stepped from behind a tree,
And with a sign beckoned follow me.
They walked to the edge of the river
And the shepherd said they would cross over
Using a euler path to an island
And then cross back to the mainland.

On their return, the place looked changed,
As if the garden were rearranged.
Directly ahead of the two walkers
Was the mansion of teachers and solvers.

The mansion is large, but its proportions
Lend it grace. Reflecting pools and fountains
Surround it, and lush vegetation
Perfumes the air with sweet scents of jasmine.
From the island, music from an octette
Drifts across the water. Geometric
Tonal paintings offer us a pallete
Of serenity, peace and quiet.

Note, as we pass the entry barrier
Words inscribed by an ancient carver:
All things are numbers still guides our work here,
As we strive for progress in other Spheres.
Residents of the pavilion may be
In the thousands, perhaps as many
As fifty thousand arranged loosely

By a hierarchy of contributions
Made prior to arrival or solutions
Developed at the research fountain
And confirmed in the gymnasium.
Important persons of unusual promise
Or those who exhibit a clever aptness
Are invited to stay. Those with Erdos
Numbers higher that seven cannot cross
The island and reside at the mansion,
Until they have made a contribution.

Please notice the mansion's courtyard entry.
On the facade there is a large marquee
Which displays the names of residents,
Lists the teachers accepting new students,
Announces the winners of games and contests,
And lists schedules of qualifying tests.
As you can tell, this is an active place.
We try to keep an energetic pace.

I have arranged to enter the mansion
To observe today's test preparation.
As you have not passed your entrance test,
We can observe only as a guest.
As we enter the grand rotunda, pause
And observe the massive Sculpture of Laws.
It depicts our work and conveys
Plans and hopes for future discoveries.
Do you not think it an impressive bronze?
It is our most treasured icon.

There are multiple halls emanating
From the rotunda. These are frustrating.
Access may be closed. Longevity
May be a factor or seniority.

Today, we are allowed to walk in this hall
And observe through the kitchen window all
Of the research and activities
Of proofs in the puddings or new theories
Established by resident teachers
And operated on by expert solvers.

I think you might enjoy some examples,
And here are some excellent samples.
Here we can see two men flipping pennies.
Pascal and Fermat are keeping tallies
To create probability tableaus
For trips to interstellar casinos.

Here Zeno is facing a paradox.
His contestant is in the starting blocks,
But so far he has refused to run,
Even though he has heard the starter's gun.
Across the hall, two Bernoulli brothers
Work on formulas for baseball players.
They want to enhance the curve on a ball
In time for a series this fall.

Many of our clients need a workplace,
So we created a Hilbert space
Where they hear vibrating harmonics
And explain music with mathematics.

Here we offer three train rides on Amtrak.
The Euclidean speeds on parallel tracks
And never crashes into other trains
Because they stay in parallel lanes,
Side by side on tracks that never merge,
Nor on speeding trains that never diverge.

Taking a ride on the Hyperbolic
Makes no sense. One sends you to the Arctic;
Track Two lets you off at the Equator.
If you need to know why, ask the conductor.

In costume, he looks like a magician.
Truth told, he is a mathematician.

Riding the Elliptic is dangerous.
Should you go, increase your insurance.
Both tracks converge light years from the station.
Destroying passenger cars and engines.

JOHN KERR

We received a present, not long ago,
Of numbers and a Mole from Avogadro
Who told us that his neighbor's garden
Has the same number of moles—a lesson
Perhaps? He asked us to examine
His mole and help him state a position.

Then he asked us to an experiment
Dealing with issues of random movement.
Without giving it much thought, we agreed
And ended up dirty and bloodied.

To and fro, back and forth and leaned on
Beneath a large balloon on the Brown's lawn.
We pushed it left; others pushed it right;
We kept pushing throughout the night.
The balloon bounced in random patterns,
Then moved in unpredictable directions,
Until captains Avogadro and Einstein
Called a time out for cheese and wine.

We may be asked to do this again,
Possibly as soon as next weekend,
But with no calendar, weeks or months,
It could be as little as a trillion seconds.

The shepherd then terminated the tour
And led the prodigy out a side door.
They walked for a while beside a stream
She heard him speaking as if in a dream.
Your test is to reaffirm a theorem
In the other place. Then we will welcome
You to the garden with full membership

When you return on a solver's starship.
You are to prove the Pi Thagorean
Theorem by inserting yourself between
The major candidates in the election
Of nineteen twelve. Using the selection
Of President by electoral votes
You are to make sure the theorem promotes
Standard practice with no visible flaws

And keeps itself within theorems and laws.

They arrived at the space-time station,
And after they set the destination,
The prodigy waved and departed
For the place where she earlier started.

He decided to wait by the river,
His toes making wavelets in the water.
He drifted away in peaceful slumber,
Thinking about everything is numbers.
When he awoke, she was standing above
Him. They had been sharing a dream of love.
They both knew it was based on joint
Respect and deeply shared scholarship:
Two disciples of mathematical
Life, joined as one in something noble.

As she began to tell him her story
She developed the history
Of the presidential elections
And the process of party selections.
She told of how ex-President Teddy
Roosevelt made William Taft his ready
Replacement then turned against him and
Failing to win the nomination ran
As a third candidate of the Bull Moose
Party. Republicans were reduced
To choosing between Taft and Roosevelt.
Woodrow Wilson, the third nominee, felt
The chances for a Democratic President
Were good; probabilities were excellent.

She continued: I decided to set
Roosevelt, Taft, and Wilson adjacent
One another in a right triangle,
And using their votes, construct a trial
To determine if Pi Thagorean
Theorems hold or if they need reworking.

I established the Bull Moose as Alpha
And the Hippopotamus as Beta.

JOHN KERR

They meet positioned orthogonal
To each other like a married couple
Who never share healthy young passion.
All communication has been broken.
Alpha stands erect, attempting to trap
Beta who lies prone and attempts to nap.
The Bull Moose claims he is for a square deal,
While the Hippo searches for his next meal.

I gave the slope of HippoPotO'Moose
To Wilson. He was concerned a truce
Might develop between fiery Alpha
And the tiring and frustrated Beta.

Results of the election were tallied,
And Woodrow Wilson won as predicted.
Woodrow Wilson won forty states;
Taft and Roosevelt combined for eight.
It was in the popular count that I
Tested. I wanted to see it comply
With the ground rules Pi Thagoras had set.
On the first count, it worked. The duet
Scored four million squared for Alpha
Three million squared for distraught Beta;
Joyous HippoPotO'Moose claimed
Five million votes verifying our test.
Squares of Alpha and Beta totaled
HippoPotO'Moose's total squared.
Then a strange thing happened to the count.
The numbers changed and began to mount.
Wilson came in at six, while Roosevelt
Stayed at four, and William Taft redealt
A three. Clearly something had happened.
Magically, one leg had lengthened.
Wilson's followers wanted a landslide
And were attempting to add to their side
Votes. Relieved my proof was still intact,
I completed my work and back tracked
To here. I did not change the vote total.
Wilson counted his five as final.
As soon as I corrected the angle,
I affirmed the Law of Right Triangles.

Well done, the shepherd exclaimed.
Pi Thagoras's Theorem is acclaimed
Again, as a fundamental canon
In heaven's mathematical garden.

Let us follow this euler path across
The island where a group works on chaos
Theories, and move to the breakfast buffet.
You look hungry. It has been a long day.

On our way, please hold my hand and listen
To an old musical definition
Of the life of a mathematician.

* * * *

Final Lecture

Lie in state for this final lecture,
Brave, supremely intelligent creature.
For your gifts to mankind, we bear witness:
We are here to praise your life and service.

The nation, your friends and family,
All people who loved democracy,
Join together as one to say farewell
To one who shielded us from the powerful.

As teacher and president at Princeton,
You helped upgrade the institution.
You led as Governor and President
With insight, compassion, and good judgment.
You guided us through a terrible war
With all of its devastating horror.

Our daughters give thanks for your courage
In supporting universal suffrage.
Blessed child of your Presbyterian
Ancestors, heritage, and tradition,
Rest easy. Leader for lasting peace.
May angel wings guide your earthly release.

* * * *

WARREN G. HARDING

President 1921-1923

Robert Introduces the Harding Poems

I met President Harding when he came to
Washington as a Senator from Ohio
And called to pay his respects at the
White House. He entered politics and
Rose through the ranks. At the convention in
Nineteen twelve, he remained loyal to
The Party and supported Taft over
Roosevelt and his Bull Moose defection.

In the Senate, he was influenced
By opponents of Wilson's Treaty
Which would commit America to the
Proposed League of Nations. Senator
Henry Cabot Lodge led Republican
Dissent, and Harding spoke against the plan.

Harding was the first President of the
Century born following the Civil
War. As President, he was popular.
He died unexpectedly while touring
Alaska and the West Coast. We laid out
His body in the White House as we had
Done for McKinley. After his passing
A series of political scandals
Captured the attention of the press
Which caused harm to his reputation.

I destroyed many letters and poems
Written to him and about him which I
Felt could make his friends uncomfortable.
I choose to remember the good in man
And know that he is a part of God's plan.

* * * *

Listening to Senator Harding

President Wilson was touring the West,
Presenting his case for the League as best
He could. He faced such opposition
That he went directly to the nation.

Senator Henry Cabot Lodge sent around word
That Senator Harding would speak and be heard
On the Treaty and declare his opposition
To anything that might weaken the nation.

I asked for permission to attend.
The gallery was packed to the brim.
As Senator Harding rose to begin,
It was very clear no one would defend
In the name of honor, flag or duty
Wilson and his encumbering treaty.

Harding's speech received tumultuous applause.
Effectively, it ended Wilson's cause.

* * * *

Warren Harding campaigning in 1920

High Stakes.
President Warren Harding plays poker with Henry Ford, Thomas Edison, Attorney General Henry Daugherty and George Getz, a man of importance from Chicago. On the table is a bottle of Canadian Rye Whiskey which Getz brought to Harding as a gift.

Senator Harding Addresses the Senate

September 11, 1919

I thank you for this opportunity
To speak to you, esteemed Senators,
On a matter of gravest importance
And share my views on our independence.

The issues before us are our reservations
To the Treaty of the League of Nations.
President Wilson is touring the West
Attempting to gain support and wrest
From us, in the name of democracy,

This dangerous, encumbering Treaty.
Secret agreements against Germany
Cannot be our responsibility.

Before he left on his tour, he hurled
We are breaking the heart of the world.
Two weeks ago, he told us to put up
(To stop debating and vote) or shut up.
I know that was a serious blunder.
Our citizens will never surrender.

This is our unending call of duty:
Pass our nation, built on integrity,
To children of the next generation,
A free, bold, and unfettered nation.

Halt the madness now. Listen to my voice,
And stop Wilson from flogging this dead horse.
I urge you to reject this concoction.
It weakens the structure of our nation.
I thank the gallery for their applause
And welcome them to our noble, just cause.

* * * *

It Was Cold on Inauguration Day

We helped President Wilson into
The carriage, covered him with a blue
Blanket to ward against the morning chill,
And sent him off toward Capitol Hill
To attend Harding's inauguration
And then return for a final luncheon.
No one could dream as they left to cheers,
Harding would be dead in less than three years.

* * * *

Thoughts on Inauguration Day

A Sonnet

Formal ceremonies begin at noon.
For this twenty-ninth inauguration.
From the Capitol we hear marching tunes.
Wilson is as dead as his League of Nations.
Our silk hats glisten in the morning air.
All covered up, he looks crumpled.
He is burdened. I have not a care.
I am strong, virile. He is withered.
He never recovered from his stroke.
Under blankets, this dying man is cold.
In our carriage, he wears a heavy cloak.
His illness made him prematurely old.

Bunting and musical compositions
Enhance these political transitions.

* * * *

Dealing From the Bottom of the Deck

For some time, I had lived a double
Life. Senator Henry Cabot Lodge had
Done several favors for me with no
Expectation other than to tell him
From time to time what was happening at
The White House that might have impact on the
Business of the Senate. He asked
That I keep my eyes open and let him
Know who was visiting or had access.
Our conversations were discreet.

As the Republican convention drew
Near in Summer of June Nineteen Twenty,
I was asked by a political
Aide of President Wilson if
I would be interested in going
To the convention as an informal
Observer. It was known that over the

Years I had many former connections
In the party, and I would raise no concerns
If I were to attend the convention.

Secretly, I passed the word to Senator Lodge
Of my opportunity, and he was
Delighted. Once there I was to report
To him and do his bidding as needed.

I arrived in Chicago on a
Late train, and even though it was late in
The evening, it was brutally hot in
The hotel. It was uncomfortable.
Cigar smoke hung in the air, and shouts at
All hours of the night made sleep difficult.

My assignment was to manage the suite
Of Colonel Harvey at the Blackstone.
I spent five days arranging for liquor,
Food, and cigars to be delivered
To the suite. I delivered notes to
Party bosses and rival candidates
On behalf of the King Makers who were
In and out of the suite at all hours.

From time to time, Harry Daughtery who
Was working behind the scenes for Harding
Would be there. Senators and Congressmen
Moved in and out of the suite. At first
It looked as if General Wood might
Win, but he could never get sufficient
Votes to break the deadlock between him and
Governor Frank Louden of Illinois.
Daughtery's plan all along was to have
Harding as each delegate's second choice.

The delegates were hot and running out
Of money. Everyone wanted it
To be over. Harding was selected
Late Saturday and became nominee
When Louden gave up his opposition.

Will Hayes and Harry Daughtery played
Their hands on behalf of Harding
With the consummate skill of river boat
Gamblers who took a bad deal at poker
And bluffed it into a winning hand.

* * * *

*Harding with important business leaders Henry Ford,
Thomas Edison and Harvey Firestone in 1920.*

Poker at the Republican Convention
The Convention Selects Warren Harding,
June 12, 1920

A Pair of Jacks*, Irvin Kirkwood,
Kansas City Star, Saturday 5:30 a.m.*

Listen to me Will Hayes. Warren Harding
Will be the Republican nominee
Because of the insight and timing
Of you and your friend, Harry Daughtery.

In Colonel Harvey's suite at the Blackstone,
(I have been told by my best informers)

At two am in a smoke filled room,
Harding was the choice of the King Makers.

Wild Card: *George Harvey, Editor*
North American Review, Saturday 3:00 a.m.

Warren, is there is any impediment
To disqualify you as candidate,
Or make or render you expedient
And exclude you from being President?

The Dealer, *Senator Henry Cabot Lodge*
Saturday 3:00 p.m.

We started this morning, and it is hot.
The delegates want to leave by Sunday.
After five roll calls, we are in a deadlock.
They are exhausted and out of money.

As convention chair, I will call a recess
(No candidate will raise, pass, fold, or call)

And try to conclude this game of chance
By reshuffling our cards in the Hall.

Folds: *Frank Louden, Governor of Illinois*
Saturday 6:05 p.m.

Warren Harding won the nomination
When Pennsylvania made him their choice.
On the final ballot, the convention
Stood shouting and yelling as with one voice.

Queen of Spades: *The Duchess, Mrs. Harding*
Saturday 6:45 p.m.
Everyone stands here yelling and screaming.
Conspirator Daughtery acts the host.
Lake Michigan is heated and boiling.
The Chicago River could boil a roast.

JOHN KERR

Ace of Spades: Nominee Warren G. Harding
Saturday 8:00 p.m.

My opportunity came yesterday
When Three of a Kind continued to fight.
We needed a candidate by today,
So the Bosses met late into the night.

Old Henry Lodge, that wheeler and dealer,
Kept shuffling the candidates and whiskey.
He was acting as the party's healer
While dealing on behalf of Daughtery.

By two a.m. my chips were high.
Finished with interminable waiting,
I was ready for Canadian Rye
And a round of political trading.

At the ante, I had few delegates,
Amounting to no more than a handful.
I called and went with a pair of eights
And finished with Aces full.

The total vote was larger than its parts.
As I left the rostrum, I gave a grand
Wave and a deep bow to my Queen of Hearts.
At last, I was able to show my hand.

Calvin Coolidge became my running mate.
Pit bosses gave him to the delegates.
Even though I played the table late,
The game ended. I accepted my fate.

* * * *

CALVIN COOLIDGE
President 1923-1929

Introduction: A Man of Dower Disposition

Warren Harding died in San Francisco
And because communications were slow,
It was early morning before Coolidge
Could be found to take the oath and pledge.
He was on his father's farm visiting
His family in Vermont, sleeping
Peacefully when he was awakened
And told quickly what had happened.
His father took the family Bible
And swore him in at the kitchen table.

A small man and dour of disposition,
Favoring plain speech with no oration,
He was known to be a penny pincher
Beyond frugal, and he drank no liquor.
At the White House, a place where he seldom
Had been invited or made to feel welcome,
He became known for strange behavior
By not speaking to his dinner partner.
Often he would create a sensation,
At dinners, refusing conversations
With his guests, then departing abruptly
As the guests were served dessert and coffee.

His terse method of communication
Contrasted with the mood of the nation.
In the middle of the Roaring Twenties,
A time of little restraint and excesses,
In pursuit of unsustainable patterns
Of dangerous financial speculations,
Coolidge sensed that the booming markets
Were fragile. Those caught up in the climate
Of greed and quick profits could be ruined.
Financial assets would be destroyed.

Coolidge and the first lady enjoyed
Sailing on the Potomac, I served
Them at their request, even though Sunday
Afternoons and evenings were my rest day.

After he left office, he retired
To his family home where he lived
A quiet, peaceful life. He wrote letters
To me on two occasions asking if I could
Locate specific documents, he would
Be most appreciative. I sent them
To him promptly, but I kept five poems.
One was his interpretation of a sermon.
Another was a prescient forecast
Of a future economic collapse.

While he was a man of integrity,
And spare in his words, the poem Brevity
Makes me smile. I sent the papers to him,
Received no reply and did not hear from him again.

Robert

* * * *

Sunday on the Potomac.
President and Mrs. Coolidge enjoy a sail on the Potomac after church.

Middle of the Night in Plymouth Notch, Vermont

August 3, 1923

In the middle of a summer night
On my father's farm in his simple home,
He awakened us with a kerosene light.
His rural dwelling had no telephone,
Utilities or electricity.
Word of Harding's death came by a driver
Who brought the news after a short journey
To Plymouth Notch from Bridgeport in his car.
I formed our group in a small circle,

Pausing to reflect on our new future.
I stood beside the Family Bible.

We prayed for strength in a whisper.
I began the oath following prayer.
I Calvin Coolidge do solemnly swear…

* * * *

Exegesis

You returned early from church, Calvin.
Tell me how you like the minister.
I hope you got something from his sermon
And gleaned some thoughts from our new preacher.

We have an ambitious schedule today.
I would like to hear the preacher's subject.
We sail on the Mayflower this Sunday.
Calvin, will you tell me his theme or topic?

Sin.

Since Moses in Sinai, a thesis
Often preached. Did he offer insight?
How to live a life religious?
Ways to walk and talk in Christian sunlight?

In today's sermon where did he begin?
Surely, he had a recommendation.
Calvin, tell me what he said about sin
When he addressed the congregation.

He was against it.

* * * *

The Business of America Is Business

Unparalleled opportunity
Grants each of us a bountiful harvest
And fulfills our dreams of prosperity
Beyond the hope of our economists.
For the last six years, we have witnessed

Control of the laws of economics
And wealth beyond anything we promised.
Our country's business is business.

We have a sound and growth economy.
In the world, the nation is the richest.
While keeping all things in harmony,
Our distribution of wealth is broadest,
And our standard of living is highest.
Reducing taxes and debt is our premise
To place this nation among the greatest.
Our country's business is business.

Less government grants greater liberty.
Our economy will not be harnessed

As long as we practice frugality
And self-regulation in the tempest
Of daily life. We will have the largest
Demand for goods, and our richness
Will stun the world's economic theorists.
Our country's business is business.

Our financial future glows the brightest.
Our plan for our citizens is righteous.
In business leaders, we place our trust.
Our country's business is business.

****

Advice on a Milk Bucket

It is a good idea
To get out of the way
When they want you and say:
We need you. Please, please stay.

****

Brevity

In my estimation
Your reputation
For wit and brevity
Are legendary.

I have made a wager
With that Miss Dowager.
At the end of dinner,
I will be the winner
If I can make you say
More than three words today.

So will I take the rose?
Please tell me.
Madam, you lose.

* * * *

The Coming Deluge

We have become a careless nation
Using highly leveraged assets,
To replace our work with speculation,
And create wealth from uncollectable debts.

This is a dangerous situation.
Creative financial engineering
Has pushed the stock market's expansion.
Investment is now crass gambling and betting.

Financial liquidity, once a stream
Flowing into capital formation,
Is now a torrent cascading downstream,
Composed of financial inventions.

Capital rivulets, rivers and ponds
Are nearing flood stage. Are bank's dams and lakes
Sufficient to hold bad corporate bonds
And stocks until we correct our mistakes?

JOHN KERR

If the national dams weaken
And break, then our worthless preferred stock
Will be swept away in crashing oceans
Of ruin. The Sheriff will bring the padlock.

Market gyrations between greed and fear
Are not in balance. Everyone competes
For rising pyramid stocks out of sheer
Greed. Too many own shares on Wall Street.

This cannot last. Our people's cash reserves
Have gone for material consumption.
Soon we will see the weakening of nerves
And face an economic depression.

Almighty God, You gave Noah guidance
As he prepared for a world deluge.
Save us Lord. Give us your perfect justice.
Help us to find a harbor and refuge.

* * * *

HERBERT HOOVER
President 1929-1933

James Opens the Old Leather Box

This leather box needs no explanation
Except to say, by way of introduction,
It was given to me by my father
Who filled it with poems and papers
He collected during the years he worked
Here in the White House. Now that I am done,
It is my plan to give it to my son
And let him continue the tradition:
Collecting poems from each administration.

* * * *

The Old Man Resumes Speaking

My attendant told me you had called
With dates for our talks to be renewed
So I had my attendants search my files
For notes from the '30s to the '60s.
Now I am better prepared to review
Leaders of that period and discuss
The career of James who replaced Robert
In the White House, James's hard work and effort
To improve himself, and his alliance
With Lyndon Johnson showed brilliance.

As Johnson accumulated power,

Johnson used James as an insider
Who fed him gossip and information
On his rivals. James gave Johnson
What he wanted, and as his unnamed
Special Agent, he was rewarded
With promotions from the 1940s
Until Johnson gave up in the '60s.
Although I cannot prove this, it is my
Belief that James helped the FBI
As well. He may have had other clients,
Those who considered him their agent.
Certainly magazines and newspapers
Would pay handsomely for juicy rumors.

James, Robert's son, was born in 1904
And began working at age 24
As an apprentice garage mechanic
Ambitious, he left that job quickly
When he got a position as a truck driver,
And then worked as Hoover's chauffer.
Hoover enjoyed James and gave him work
Serving houseguests and as a filing clerk.
Over time, James's responsibilities
Increased. He went on to work forty-one
Years, surviving the traumatic transition
To Roosevelt after his election.
Roosevelt put so much blame on Hoover,
That James became a Democratic donor
And made himself useful to Eleanor.

James became Roosevelt's valet,
Then became his arms, legs, and confidant.
James walked with Truman to take the oath
Of office when Roosevelt passed. Both
Men agreed that James should stay on staff
And work in the White House on his behalf.
James worked for Truman and transitioned
To the Eisenhowers when they moved
In. His most pleasant job was caddying
For President Eisenhower, helping
Him line up his putts at Congressional.
For a few short years, the Presidency
Was marked with a new intensity

JOHN KERR

When John Kennedy and his family
Roared into the White House, infusing
It with vitality and capturing
The hearts of the American public.
Then it ended in televised tragic
Horror. Vice President Johnson, never
A friend of the President's brother,
Was shunned flying back to Washington.

Hoover, *a confident leader and executive at his desk.*

James drove to Langley to meet *Air Force One*
With letters of condolence and bourbon.
James worked until Lyndon retired
And moved to Texas. James followed,
Driving Johnson around the Hill Country,
Then working in Austin at the Library.
He told stories of working for Johnson
And gave lectures on life in Washington.

✦✦✦✦

James Speaks of His Life in Washington

Good afternoon to distinguished guests,
Faculty and friends. Your presence suggests
That you think I might bring new insights
Of my forty years with six Presidents.
Sadly, at my advancing age, I may
Be guilty of repeating myself today,
But I will try to present new stories
And read poems from those years and hope they please
And entertain you. Certainly some dates
Are wrong, and you may be frustrated,
But I ask you to enjoy the story
And forgive my incorrect history.
The lyrics may be inaccurate and wrong.
Please, just hum the melody of this song.

* * * *

James's Sonnet: On His Retirement

Thank you for those heartfelt speeches and toasts
Which give me strength to face my retirement.
In my forty years here, I have heard almost
Every toast, but tonight I, your servant,
Stand here to express my deep gratitude
To you my friends for your thoughtfulness.
Because of you, I have a renewed
Commitment to our national purpose.

I have served magnates, liars, and senators
And greeted each with a respectful smile.
They considered me their personal butler,
As I cleaned their toilets with a sense of style.

Serving others we keep our future bright.
Thank you my friends for coming tonight.

* * * *

James Describes Hoover

As a student at Stanford University
Hoover majored in Geology,
Then went to work internationally.
Successful and a millionaire at forty,
He wanted to do something for humanity.
Because of the Great War with Germany,
Starvation was near in western countries.
A believer in personal charity,
He took a job helping Europe's hungry.
Noticed for his selfless generosity,
His star began rising politically.

He served as Commerce Secretary
For Harding and Coolidge in the '20s.
Hoover followed the Efficiency
Movement which held that in society
Individuals make the economy
Function better. Governments are guilty
Of built in waste and inefficiencies.

After Coolidge ceased his candidacy,
Hoover entered the primaries,
Running on Republican Prosperity.
With his personal popularity,
He won the '28 election easily.

Thinking he could end widespread poverty
And feed the nation's poor and hungry,
He raised taxes on the wealthy.
An isolationist in foreign policy,
He resolved conflict between Peru and Chili,
Forcing them to sign a long-term treaty.

A year into Hoover's presidency,
A worldwide depression hit the country.
Unable to produce economic recovery,
Democrats seized the opportunity,
Making Hoover the face of failed policies.

Roosevelt won the office in '33,

Using attacks on Hoover's personality
As a guiding political philosophy,
He called him an instrument of the wealthy,
Insensitive, a monstrosity
Who stood on the neck of humanity.
To bring needed relief to the country,
There were points on which they could agree,
But Roosevelt wanted no one to see
Hoover other than Simon Legree.

Roosevelt kept the people in misery
Through the Interregnum, then in an irony
Of politics, implemented many
Of Hoover's plans for recovery.

A portrait of Hoover by Howard Christy
Displays his pain from this tragedy.
It is in the Hoover Library
At Stanford University.

* * * *

Statism

It appears that this administration
Is replacing individualism
With reliance on Central Statism
To create a Socialistic nation.

I ask: what is the role of government?
Is the state the be all and the end all
Of man? If so, it will be our downfall.
We dare not reject our Founders' judgment.

Our freedom from the State is the envy
Of all peoples. I cannot see the wisdom
Of encouraging collective action,
And sacrifice personal liberty.

This economic turmoil will not last

Forever, and when it has ended
Liberty must remain unchallenged
When this Depression has passed.

I implore you to exercise caution.
Offer a helping hand with charity.
Help feed the poor through generosity.
Firmly reject the Socialist's poison.

* * * *

Interregnum by FDR

Please accept my heartiest congratulations
For your committee's staff press relations
Effort spearheaded by Charles Mickelson.

Your thoughtful strategy of portraying
Hoover as a miserly, cruel, uncaring
Despot has the electorate seething.

His bold symbol of an empty wallet
And keeping Hoover as the sole target
Caused confidence in him to plummet.

Hoover's ethics formed as a Quaker
Account for his political failure
To fight against our unfounded rumors.

Lies, false charges and vilification
Make him an object of derision.
Should we inspire men or win elections?

We will keep holding him responsible
For actions that are reprehensible
Until all think he is contemptible.

We will spike publications with poison
To explain how men's futures were stolen,
Making Hoover the face of high treason.

I will widen the personal chasm

Between us during the interregnum,
Blaming him solely for the Depression.

After the swearing in, I will not meet
With him again. Shunning will be complete.
As Scapegoat, he will taste lifelong defeat.

Let me affirm our future strategy:
We are not here to create a better society
Or encourage greater civility.

Our voters should see themselves as failures.
We are not here to lift up or inspire.
Our job is to win and retain power.

FDR

* * * *

Living in a Hoover Hotel

I'm living in a Hoover hotel
Down by the railroad track.
It's only a makeshift shack,
But I'm not going back.

I lost a good job at the cotton gin,
Sweeping floors for a dime.
I sing to pass the time;
Hunger is not a crime.

A man sold me a sack of pinto beans,
With two cups of coffee,
Soon everyone will see
The joys of living free.

I have a brother who went to New York
From our little village.
He works hauling garbage
And sleeps under a bridge.

My sister lives on a Red River farm,

Married to a sharecropper
Who left Oklahoma
For California.

*Soon everyone will see
The joys of living free.*

* * * *

Musings While My Time Runs Out

In my time, I have seen many Senators,
Congressmen, and Cabinet Officers,
And eight Presidents laid out with honors.
I must say I miss some more than others.

Teddy Roosevelt had great energy
And compelled everyone to agree
With him. He opposed Taft unwisely
And damaged the Republican Party.

Roosevelt thought that William Howard Taft
Was his ideal successor and drafted
Him. Once Taft was elected he chaffed
Under the yoke. I never saw him laugh.

At the start of the War, I helped Wilson
Feed Americans trapped in London,
Then organized relief for Belgium
With large public and private donations.

We were ready for a man like Harding:
Handsome, pleasant, but he was a sporting
Man. Some in his cabinet were dealing
Improperly. Then they were caught stealing.

I got the nomination when Coolidge
Gave mixed signals right up to the edge
Of the convention, later alleging
That I caused him personal damage.

Class warfare was FDR's philosophy.

He pitted the poor against the wealthy.
He preached that the glass was half-empty
As a way to keep the voters unhappy.

I was honored by Harry Truman,
A man who made difficult decisions
On behalf of a war-weary nation.
He could withstand the heat of the kitchen.

He was followed by Eisenhower
Who made the transition to our leader
From the position of victorious soldier
And guided us through a period of danger.

A light went out when we had to bury
Our young President, John F. Kennedy.
Then later we lost his brother Bobby
Setting awry our national story.

The treacherous act of a mad gunman
Launched the presidency of Lyndon Johnson
Who fought for Civil Rights, as the nation
Turned against the war in Vietnam.

Goldwater and Johnson are campaigning.
I endorsed Goldwater, while knowing
He has no possibility of winning.
The Democrats see a landslide coming.

They have planned a state service for me,
Complete with fine flowers and eulogies.
Then transport me to West Bend to bury
Me next to Lu in the cemetery.

* * * *

Fishing Stories

Herbert Hoover enjoyed fishing stories,
Jokes on the one that got away,
Tall tales of ritual bait recipes,
Or the one about the woman praying

For Divine Intervention. There are more
Fishing tales than fish in the seven seas,
And Hoover kept his share of angling lore.

Fly casting along the Russian River
Or fishing the Merced in Yosemite,
While camping out in the Mariposa
Beneath the giant sequoia trees,
Gave him perspective and a metaphor
For judging Presidents in the modern
Era. Asked to explain his concerns,
He answered: *Coolidge fished with worms.*

* * * *

On the Russian River

Joining

Oars are at rest; we glide on the current.
The river is dark in the late afternoon.
In my pouch, flies comfort one another.
One, the Coachman, has a story to tell.

Early morning, he went low and tempted
A Steelhead. Turning, it took him away.
Coachman was not going to lose the fight.
Rod, reel, line and Coachman took the Steelhead.

Separating

A Blue Heron ignores us as we pass.
His gaze is upon the water ahead.
Red Wing Blacks chatter over a grievance.
Mergansers run to flight ahead of us.

Our guide will be on the river at dawn.
Coachman may be selected tomorrow.
The Steelhead will swim to his fate upriver.
We leave for home to meet our fates as well.

* * * *

Early Morning in Yosemite on the Merced River

Morning on the Merced. Peaceful, Quiet.
Towering above us, Granite Sentries
Guarding Mirror Lake and the Merced.
Turning leaves of yellow-gold at sunrise.

Pulling on waders at the River's edge,
Assembling fly rod, attaching reel,
Opening a fly box of Romanov jewels,
Nominating coy temptress candidates.
Selecting the right fly among many.
Anticipating the day. Quickening pulse.

Entering the River. A strong current.
Wading slowly. Feeling the crunch of gravel.
Rising above me, a desperate Hatch,
Seeking mates in reproductive frenzy.
Waiting below, Rainbows ready themselves.

Continuing downstream. Slippery bottom.
Scanning, watching the surface for signals.
Loading the line to three o'clock. Pausing.
Casting to the boulder near the far bank,
Arching the line up and out to the target,
Presenting the fly gently above the rock.
Watching the fly drift past the boulder.

Hitting hard. Setting the hook. Running.
Stripping the line. Coming at me. Reeling.
Running hard again. Line is singing.
Tiring. The Rainbow is tiring. Tip up.
Bringing him in close, final struggle.

Netting him in the morning light.
Glistening, white shiny scales, clear eyes.
Smelling the sweet scent of nature's creation.
Holding him in my hands, then releasing.
Returning him gently to the River.
Watching him pause, then gliding away.

Morning on the River. Peaceful. Quiet.

Towering above us. Granite Sentries
Guarding Mirror Lake and the Merced.
Turning leaves of yellow-gold. Deep blue sky.

Intervening in the cycle of life.
Praising our God for His gift of fishing.

****

Camping Beneath the Giant Sequoias

In magic Northern California,
We camp in this grove of Giant Sequoia.
High above, the Redwoods form a canopy
That shields us from the world's reality.
Early fog makes this a mystical place,
A setting for insight in quiet space.
At noon, I will take a leisurely walk
Through the trees for my final lakeside talk.
Today, I saw an owl consume a spider
Overhead, near last night's campfire.

Camping helps us heighten our senses
Until our time when the music ceases.

****

On the Russian River
Herbert Hoover casts a fly for a Steelhead near the Bohemian Grove encampment on the Russian River. The poem "On the Russian River" recounts the cast.

FRANKLIN D. ROOSEVELT
President 1933-1945

James Was Off to a Bad Start

Sunrise on March fourth, nineteen thirty-three
Was the start of a dreadful day for me.
It was the day of inauguration
For Franklin Roosevelt's administration,
And it had been told to us who worked
Here that he was a man who despised
All persons who had associated
With Herbert Hoover and Republicans.
To continue, we would need to make amends.

On the first day, we worked quietly, hoping
No one would notice us and avoiding
Eye contact when we stumbled into
One of his political retinue.
It worked. We survived the first days,
And I began to help them in ways
Which made them recognize that my service
Was important, and I could keep secrets.

After a year, they trusted me and sought
My counsel. They insisted I be brought
Along when he traveled to assist
Or carry him because his legs were useless

From Polio. He was paralyzed
Below the waist. He was drawn and withered.

The press helped maintain the deception
That he had conquered his affliction.
In a parade he would stand in a car
And hold tight to a special handle bar.

I worked for him for twelve years, helping
Him with simple tasks, delivering
Messages, answering correspondence.
I like to think I had some influence.

Depressions, World Conflict, Domestic Strife
Caused upheavals to the way of life
We knew before his Presidency.
We were forging a new identity.

A reporter asked me to name a trip
I remember most. It was to Egypt
For a third meeting with Winston Churchill
On Lake Bitters near the Suez Canal
After meetings with Stalin at Yalta.
There he met with Abdulazziz of Arabia,
King Farouk of Egypt and Haile Selassie,
The influential ruler of Ethiopia.

Roosevelt was suffering from coronary
Disease having lived an unhealthy
Lifestyle for years. He returned home to address
The Congress and then to Warm Springs to rest.
His physicians were sure he was dying.
We could not accept his days were ending.

He never returned from Georgia,
But his friend from South Carolina,
Lucy Mercer Rutherford came to visit
And brought a friend to paint his portrait
Which was never finished. To help hide
Lucy's presence, she decided to drive
Them back to Aiken before he passed.
They were driving when he took his last breath.
Before he died, I left for Washington
To be there to make preparations
For the public viewing and funeral
And the trip to Hyde Park for burial.

Deception

Horror seized me at Campobello.
My legs, once powerful, became lifeless.

I was diagnosed with polio
And doomed to a life of helplessness.
Braces, crutches, canes and a special wheelchair
Marked me as a permanent invalid.
Hiding appliances of my nightmare,
I refused to be seen as tethered.
I learned to bend others to my will.
To most, I appear as a complete human.
In public, I appear healthy and virile.
It is an orchestrated deception.
Photographs of my wheel chair are never kept.
The White House press corps protects my secret.

✶✶✶✶

A rare photograph of Roosevelt in a wheelchair.

POEMS AND SONGS OF THE PRESIDENTS OF THE 20TH CENTURY

A Fireside Chat.
Franklin Roosevelt completes one of his radio broadcasts to the American people. These broadcasts brought reassurance to people who were trying to recover from the Depression. Roosevelt believed he was a great actor and communicator.

Revising the Party

Uniting America's downtrodden,
We have reconstructed our old party.
Establishing a new coalition,
We won a political victory.
We appeal to men saddled with debt
And those who join organized labor:
Men whose scant wages are earned by sweat,
Miners, construction workers and farmers.
We enroll minorities and ethnics,
Control the South and the inner city.
Intellectuals, Jews and Catholics
Drive our urban voting machinery.
Our enemies are mine owners, bankers,
Capitalists, financiers and lenders.

* * * *

We Interred Japanese Americans

One of the war's domestic tragedies
Was internment of Japanese Americans
In places of bitter cold like Heart Mountain
And the stifling summers of Tucson.
In fear, their properties were seized
By friends and allies of the President.

A White House doctor, Edward Murphy,
Who had treated internees in Arizona,
Gave me this Haiku by Hirabayashi
Which laments his unfair circumstance.

James

* * * *

Hirabayashi

hitchhike to Tucson
yellow pine to saguaro
find the honor camp

moonlight shadows help
sparkling diamond necklaces
mark sentry borders
by day we build roads
coyote howls in the night
remove the ocean.

* * * *

Thoughts

Tucson-Tucson-two sons I thought. My place now.
Language new two for many. Why?
Parents' tongue and name hushed.
Driven here confused.
Honor Camp called.
Lost, I come here.

Dark night, shadow moon thrown
On road and path dust dry.
Day and night a cry comes,
Fenced object foreign.

Here, far from Pacific's sound,
I live dead too much, stay, wait.

Hirabayashi

* * * *

Correspondence November 1940

My dear Mr. President, as we reach
The last month of this terrible year, each
Night brings new hardships to endure.

Our people can withstand the nightly slaughter,
But we now face the situation
Of an economic strangulation.
A turning point in the war approaches.
We are short on supplies and finances.
Dozens of factories are damaged;
The House of Commons is devastated.
We will not shrink from any sacrifice,
Nor shirk from paying the ultimate price
With our blood to save our population.

We are in a perilous situation;
We need assistance to save our nation.

Churchill

My Dear Prime Minister, you strike
A raw nerve when you tell us the third Reich
Is at your doorstep. Your letter came by
Seaplane to our ship off Cuba. May I
Begin by saying that you and England
Are in our constant thoughts. A threatened,
Then conquered England, will have direct
Impact on our country. Left unchecked
The Axis powers will bring this terrible war
To the American eastern seashore.

On this cruise (part work and part vacation),
I outlined a new formulation:
We will keep the British Isles from falling
With a program of lending and leasing
For whatever you deem as essential
To keep Germany across the channel.

We will reopen closed factories
To make weapons for the Allied Armies.
We will send food, supplies, arms, medicines,
Tanks, planes, ships, rifles and ammunition.
America will be known as the Land of the Free
And the Arsenal of Democracy.

I have a metaphor for this concept

Which makes it easy for all to accept.
If there is a fire at your neighbor's house,
You lend him a spare hose so he can douse
The fire before the flames reach your residence:
That is neighborly interdependence.

Franklin

* * * *

Winston Churchill, Roosevelt and Joseph Stalin at Yalta.
Roosevelt died two months later.

Enter Stage Left

I think of myself as a great actor.
America is my personal stage.
I can move an audience to laughter,
Or send it home with shouts of bitter rage.
The country thinks it knows me. Radio
Broadcasts carry my personal message
Of hope for a better tomorrow
And my commitment to a living wage.

My stage entrances are rehearsed.
I flash a smile and wave my fedora.
The wheel chair is never photographed.
My main prop is my cigarette holder.
I insist they play Pomp and Circumstance
At the end of each performance.

* * * *

Save Me, God of Abraham
Be merciful to me, O Lord, for I am weak;
Heal me, my very bones are shaken.

We had been sitting in freezing drizzle
For two hours, guarded by sullen boys
In dirty uniforms. Now we stumble
Forward. I hold the child's hand. There is noise
Up ahead of us. Smells of smoke, urine,
And vomit drift through the haze. Odors
Of death and decay reach us. Broken
Spirits keep moving to avoid the Stranglers.

How long, O Lord, wilt thou quite forget me?
How long wilt thou hide thy face from me?

Men with pushcarts and wagons trail behind
Us as we shuffle toward the showers.
I know where they are taking us. My mind
Foresees deadly toxins, not cleansing waters.

My heart has turned to wax and melts within me.
My mouth is dry as a potsherd,
And my tongue sticks to my jaw;
I am laid low in the dust of death.

The pace quickens. A gate closes. We pass
Into a packed room. The lights dim. Death
Swallows me. Eyes and lungs sear from the gas.
I lose my will, my life. I lose my breath.

* * * *

1943

We met three times in 1943
To plan the war against Adolph Hitler
And his allies Japan and Italy.
We agreed to fight the Nazi Furher,
Defeat the Axis, then turn on Asia.
We erased and then redrew boundaries
With help from Brandy and Russian vodka,
Carved up empires and made new countries.
I know I charmed that old bear Stalin
With my poking fun at Winston Churchill.
I got his pledge and promise in Tehran
By using my humor, charm and goodwill.
Next year Stalin will host us in Yalta,
A seaside resort on the Crimea.

* * * *

Lucy

I want her with me when I die.
She and I shared our lives in secret.
As I have grown infirm, I must rely
On her, sitting for my formal portrait.
We live balanced on a tightrope.
Shielded from discovery from my wife,
Lucy brings the joy of sunshine and hope
In these last days of my life.

Eleanor drove her into the shadows.
For three days I have thought in silence.
She left disgraced, returned a widow.
I know she is near. I feel her presence.
I am dying. I must see Lucy's face.
Bring her to me for a final embrace.

* * * *

HARRY S. TRUMAN
President 1945-1953

Truman Becomes President

They sent me to fetch the Vice President
And explain to him that it was urgent
That he should report immediately
To the White House and go directly
To the family quarters. Truman sensed
That President Roosevelt had died.
On our way we passed Lyndon Johnson,
The Texas protégé of Sam Rayburn,
Who waved to us and flashed his grin.
Roosevelt was gone; Truman soon sworn in;
Johnson is scheming and planning his future
Under the guidance of the House Speaker.

Truman was not well-known when he became
President and was treated with contempt and disdain
By Republicans and his own party.
He was regarded as a caretaker,
A product of political machinery,
With no prayer of being a leader.

He surprised us with his determination
And perseverance. He led the nation
Through the end of the War and contained
The Soviet Union's expansion during

The time that became known as the Cold War,
But scandals by his appointees marred
Truman's political reputation
Threatening his bid for reelection.

When he sought reelection he was an
Underdog. No one gave him more than
A slight chance to defeat Governor
Thomas Dewey, an ex-prosecutor,
Who sported a pencil thin mustache.
Some said it was the mustache that dashed
Dewey's hopes, but what won the election
Was a cross-country train trip by Truman.

* * * *

Grandmother Truman's Lesson

Cleaning his office after he departed
For Independence, I discovered
A folder marked Grandmother's Lessons.
All the contents had been removed
Except one titled Golden Doctrines
In the handwriting of President Truman.

Remain steadfast.
Do not weaken.
If you wilt in the heat,
Get out of the kitchen.

* * * *

Truman at His Desk.
Unafraid, He is ready for the business of the day. Truman suffered from an unfriendly press and an unsympathetic electorate. He did not suffer from self doubt.

Menu for Sunday Lunch: Fried Chicken, Southern Biscuits, and Old-Fashions

During Roosevelt's administration,
The White House kitchen was deplorable.
The most simple cooking preparation
Was unappealing and tasted dreadful.

It was no secret that the dinner rolls
Prepared by Henrietta Nesbitt
Were tougher than our infantry's boot soles.
Mr. Truman told me to make her quit.

After she was gone, Elizabeth Moore
Became the cook. As soon as she was hired,
She began serving meals to restore
Appeal. Formal dinners were improved.

The Truman's made a request of the kitchen:
For lawn picnics or an informal brunch,
Include Southern biscuits and fried chicken,
And make that the standard Sunday lunch.

Mr. Truman hated hard rolls and crumpets.
He said these breads were a baking failure.
He loved to eat Southern style biscuits
Made with Wagoner's *Queen of the Pantry* flour.

Give to the cook or chef who is wise
Chicken pieces soaked (such as breasts or thighs)
In buttermilk. Then pat them almost dry
And dredge them in Queen of the Pantry flour,
Seasoned with some spice, salt and pepper.
Let them rest chilled for half an hour.
Fry them in lard in a cast iron skillet.
Transfer the chicken to a paper basket
And serve it later with buttered biscuits.

Truman's Light Southern Biscuits for Brunch

Mix two cups of Wagoner-Gates flour
With two and a half teaspoons of soda,
A cup of lard, a pinch of salt, and butter.
Combine the dry ingredients: salt, soda
With two teaspoons of baking powder.
Then add the magic Queen's Pantry flour
And lard. Then blend it all together
With a cup of buttermilk and butter.
The biscuits will be light as a feather.

Sunday Baking with an Old Fashion at Your Side

While baking, we enjoy an Old Fashion:
Put the cut biscuits in a hot oven.
Fill a glass with three ounces of bourbon
And sip slowly, contemplating Heaven
By reflecting on the preacher's sermon.

* * * *

Justification for the Use of Atomic Weapons

Sir, stop your haranguing accusations.
I agreed to meet you with the expectation
That you would engage me in conversation
On my plan to use atomic weapons
On cities in the Japanese homeland,

Instead of a military island.
So far today you have wasted my time
With baseless accusations of war crimes.

Sir, indeed you have implied as much,
And I will no longer tolerate such
Inflammatory and hostile questions.
So if you have nothing else, this session
Is terminated. Give my regards to
Your editor. I doubt that he knew
That you would abuse this invitation
To discuss those joint wartime decisions.

* * * *

Sir, yes I have received the letter
Of apology from your editor,
And given his most apologetic
Statement and the change in your rhetoric,
I will grant you the opportunity
(Unless I detect animosity)
To restart this important interview,
And in the process establish a true
And accurate account of the reasons
We decided against a massive invasion.

Sir, let me respond to your assertion
That we became an evil nation
When we used devastating weapons
On noncombatant civilians.
We are in the business of ending
Wars, not in the business of starting
Them. My task, as commander in chief,
Was to conclude the war and bring relief
To millions of people and their nations,
Suffering from the war's devastation.
The cost of an invasion would deplete
Our resources and cause us to retreat
From a leadership position
In world affairs. I made a decision
To make a showing of cataclysmic
Proportions using our new atomic
Bombs on the cities of Hiroshima
And Nagasaki. It would be a
Method to allow peace talks to surface.
Their leaders needed a way to save face.
We sent them a peace proposal, calling
For an immediate cease fire, ending
The war. Their response was unacceptable.
When they ignored our ultimatum,
We unleashed atomic Armageddon.
This was not a military error.
It was a bold act to reign terror
Until they agreed to reasonable
Terms at the negotiating table.

We did not bomb in desperation.
It was a reasoned calculation.
Japan surrendered six days after
Nagasaki. We learned much later
The vast extent of the destruction
Caused by the atom bomb's explosion.
Lost were 250,000 lives.
I brought home a million men to their wives.

Well, I see our time is at an end.
I am pleased we were able to mend
Our fences between insinuations

And ethical justifications.
I have a present for you, if I may.
A photo of the crew of the Angola Gay
Posing for the camera. Their mission
Forced Japanese capitulation.
As you depart, please observe the painting
Of our brave warriors returning.

This is my response to the controversy:
I did what I knew was necessary.

* * * *

Rising and Falling in Opinion Polls

I won reelection and was cheered
By forty-nine per cent of the nation.
The banks and Wall Street financiers feared
I would lead them into a Depression,
But I remained highly admired
Until the war in South Korea
Widened. Then I became despised
Over a potential war with China.
In Asia, America's best were dying.
Before, I was rated one of the best.
Shortly, I sank from the highest polling
Rung to the absolutely lowest.
Korea's stalemate sank my Presidency.
Someday, I will rate high in history.

* * * *

Salty Language in Independence

Please sit, and welcome to Independence.
You have come a considerable distance
For this post presidential interview.
I agreed to it because I find you
To be honest and insightful, direct
In you thinking and never circumspect
In your approach. So with that introduction,
Let us begin with your first question.

POEMS AND SONGS OF THE PRESIDENTS OF THE 20TH CENTURY

Ah, you ask for my candid assessment
Of three men with whom my disagreements
Are well known. Each was a thorny problem
For me during my administration.

We might as well start with Edgar Hoover
Who shows no appetite for jailing mobsters.
He plants stories with favored columnists
Of alleged, traitorous Communists.

When I ran for office in forty-eight,
He dug up dirt from my race for Senate.
He sent his agents to Kansas City
To exhume election discrepancies.
Unable to find anything amiss,
He tried to link me to Alger Hiss,
The Soviet spy in the State Department,
Monitored by his Special Agents.
Then he sent rumors to a sympathetic press
Which he thought would ensure Dewey's success.

After I won, he called off the witch
Hunts. I should have fired the son-of-a-bitch,
But I was too busy with world problems,
While Hoover played Spymaster Possum.

Hoover is an autocratic tyrant
Who will be exposed, for the Serpent
He is, in the future when the Bureau
Quits blackmailing Hoover's political foes.

I ran against Governor Tom Dewey
For President. A landslide victory
By him was predicted by the High Hats
Of the national press, those sewer rats
For the Republican bankers.
They portrayed Dewey as the Savior
Of all our financial problems
While ruling from their Wall Street kingdoms.

Against all odds, I pulled an upset.
See this *Tribune* headline. No one forgets
The late night news: Dewey Defeats Truman.
That headline swept Dewey into the dustpan
Of History. His inept advisors
Cost him dearly. They forgot the farmers
And the men who work and toil with their sweat,
Who live with a crushing burden of debt.

So what were my problems with Thomas Dewey,
Other than he looked like a Spanish Marquis?
With his cool demeanor and thin mustache
He looked down his nose like we were trash.
His entire appearance and slick coiffure
Reminded me of a load of manure.

I took a train and went to the people,
But he retreated and took the gamble
That he could win a sweeping election
And become President of the nation.
I beat that snooty New York attorney
With Pendergast tactics from Missouri.

My decision to fire Douglas MacArthur
Was not made lightly. He was Commander
Of the Far East, based in Tokyo,
Widely regarded as a war hero.
In Korea, he had planned and won
A surprising victory at Inchon.
His plan was to expand the war in Asia
And drop nuclear bombs on mainland China.

My goal was to negotiate a peace
Settlement with China to allow a cease
Fire at the thirty-eighth parallel.
If I had announced this goal, all hell
Would have broken out. Articles of Impeachment
Would have been launched to stop appeasement
Of international Communism.
It would have led to a deeper schism
Between our people. Called Truman's War,
The war and I became unpopular.

While we were drafting the peace proposal,
MacArthur tossed a diplomatic bombshell
At the Chinese. He sent them a proclamation
Which completely undermined our position.
He taunted them, laughing at their power
And threatened that he would expand the war.

It was outright insubordination,
As he sought a head-on confrontation,
Placing me between him and the Constitution
While forcing Congress to endorse his action.
I considered his ultimatum
For some time. After consultation
With the Joint Chiefs, Justice and State,
I concluded I could not wait,
So I fired him, bringing on condemnation
From the Press and most of the nation.

Perhaps you remember the Hero's parades,
His speech to Congress or his motorcades.
The Republicans used him to their advantage.
They launched inflammatory language,
With a constant barrage of criticism,
At me until the public found it tiresome.

Each time our delusional West Pointer
Was seen in public, a photographer
Recorded this pompous Caesar's
Daily comings and goings for dinner
With important swells or wading ashore
On vacation Isles with major donors.

What began as a traitorous tempest
Died out a year later. The public lost interest.
The Press ceased praising his bravado
And fed him to his monumental ego.
We brokered a treaty with Red China
To conclude the conflict in Korea.
Our army remains under civilian
Control as required by the Constitution.

Am I bitter because of his actions?
Let me answer your pointed question.
I enjoy seeing him politically castrated,
Even though the public remains divided.

As to your request for my frank comments
And assessments of recent Presidents,
It is now getting too late in the day
For a lengthy response, except to say
As President, Dwight D. Eisenhower
Was ineffective. He was a better golfer.
He should have spent more time in Augusta
Than Washington. Jack Kennedy
Was my favorite. His energy
Launched the nation forward with goals
That stirred his fellow countrymen's souls.

I have great respect for Lyndon Johnson
As a consummate politician.
His Great Society legislation
Was overshadowed by Vietnam.
Richard Nixon came here to Independence,
Played the piano and had enough sense
To leave early, setting a precedent
Used later when he was President.

I have enjoyed today's conversation.
You may find insight in our discussion,
But now it is time to close this session
And enjoy an afternoon Old Fashion.
It is time for you to be on your way.
Stay dry, rain is forecast later today.

∗∗∗∗

The Whistle Stop Campaign

Harry Truman won the nomination
Of the Democrats for reelection
In '48, but public opinion
Turned in favor of Thomas Dewey.

A split in the Democratic Party
Threatened to destroy its unity.
Strom Thurmond drew off southern Democrats
Into a new party of Dixiecrats
Favoring segregation and state's rights.
The Progressives led by Henry Wallace
Used the party's left wing as its base,
Injecting some confusion into the race.
As the choice of Old Guard Republicans,
Dewey appeared more fit to govern
Than the fiery, irascible Truman.
Radio and Press pundits' predictions,
And private voter polling reactions,
Said defeat was a foregone conclusion.

Truman resurrected the Whistle Stop Campaign
Of Roosevelt, using a private train,
To take him to the voters and regain
His momentum, then win the election.
The press thought the plan was desperation.
We thought it was divine inspiration.

We planned to head west to Seattle,
Tracing half of a lopsided circle.
We would make a lengthy, classic Whistle
Stop campaign, speaking out in Iowa,
Then stop in Colorado and Utah.
From Seattle to California,
Across Texas and Oklahoma,

We would be able to talk straight and tell
The voters that Republicans will bring ill
On our nation, and our lives will be hell.

We would speak our minds in San Diego
And give them hell in San Antonio,
All across the Midwest to Ohio.

While we seek to improve race relations,
Republicans will destroy the nation
With schemes for uncontrolled inflation.

We considered extending our mission
To Philadelphia, New York, and Boston,
Letting the people see Harry Truman.

We planned a tumultuous reception
In October on our return to Washington,
To bring our trip to its conclusion.

By September seventeenth our plans were set.
No person with a sane mind would bet
That Harry Truman would ever win, yet
We were hopeful. He stood on the platform
Of the train, promising a rolling firestorm
Of passionate speeches which would transform
His campaign. He would bring his family
Along. He would stress Party loyalty
And be seen as trustworthy and friendly.

With whistles blowing, we left Washington,
Lurching and grinding from Union Station
In the Ferdinand Magellan pullman.
The seventeen car Special had sleepers,
Lounges, press cars, staff quarters, and diners,

Power generators, a signal car.
Ours was a railroad odyssey
Steaming west on a Pilgrimage to see
If we could win support of the country.

We found our voice in Iowa,
Improved its delivery in Utah,
And brought it home to California.

POEMS AND SONGS OF THE PRESIDENTS OF THE 20TH CENTURY

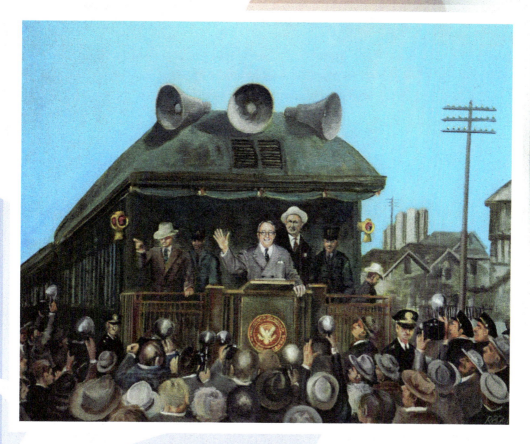

Harry Truman campaigns with Lyndon Johnson and Sam Rayburn in Texas.

We began to repeat our basic theme:
Republicans offer failed schemes
Which work against men. We help their dreams
Come true. Large crowds came from the beginning
Thinking that he had a chance of winning.
Most everyone else saw Truman losing.

At the state plowing contest in Dexter,
Truman spoke to ninety thousand farmers
In the hot swelter of Indian summer.

Remember the insurance companies
In '29 destroyed communities,
Taking thousands of farms from families.

Truman was best speaking spontaneously
To small groups, mixing sophistry

151

With large amounts of demagoguery.

Plans for price supports are in jeopardy.
They want to destroy your prosperity
And shut down your grain facilities.

He brought the attack continuously.
Attack, attack became his strategy.
Always take the fight to the enemy.
When I speak of what Republicans are doing,
I am describing their corrupt, cunning
Leaders who have become hard of hearing.

We honed our message to be clearer:
Truman needs votes from workers and farmers.
Republicans are the choice of bankers.

Republicans have a complete lack
Of interest in working men. They look
Down, then stick pitchforks in the farmer's back.

The train became part of our strategy.
We made it part of the local scenery.
Our visits were brief, and we left promptly.

Each time we arrived at a small town,
The engineer would turn the train around.
A local politician would come down
To introduce Truman. The train was fascinating
To most everyone, clanging and banging
Against itself as the band was playing.
Truman would step onto the rear platform,
Connect himself to a local person,
And launch into a condemnation
Of the Congress and the Republicans
Who did nothing for Californians,
Washingtonians, Iowans or Texans.

Then he introduced his family,
Daughter Margaret and Bess, first lady,
Who were received and greeted warmly.
Someone would tell the band to start playing

Hail to the Chief as we were departing.
Three Trumans would wave as we were leaving.

We spoke frequently in Colorado,
Spoke truth at the Mormon Tabernacle,
Blasted Republicans in Nevada.
All the way from Iowa to Seattle,
The crowds who came to see us were cordial
At each stop, but never emotional.

That changed after he spoke in Los Angeles.
The size of the crowds began to impress
Our staff and the working national Press.
At Gilmore Stadium, Ronald Reagan,
A liberal Democrat, opened
For us, and the crowd cheered for Truman.

We drew large, vocal crowds in San Diego
And pointed the train toward El Paso,
Then Uvalde to San Antonio,
Where crowds of 250,000
Cheered us on. Congressman Sam Rayburn
Got on board with Lyndon Johnson.

I say to you: You are the government.
I am only your employed servant.
More important than being President.

In one day he spoke in Austin, Belton,
San Marcos, Temple, Waco, Georgetown,
Ft. Worth and Dallas, finishing in Bonham.

Crossing the Red River into Oklahoma.
We gave them fits in towns like Eufala,
Ardmore, Shawnee, Muskogee, and Tulsa.

At one point we ran low on money,
But we raised enough in Paul's Valley
To get us to Oklahoma City.

Our problems are publicity seeking
Politicians who will not help housing

Or help out on problems that need solving.

He spoke to large crowds in Oklahoma,
He spoke out in Kentucky and Missouri,
With huge turnouts in West Virginia.

The Press gave us no chance of victory.
His homespun speeches were seen as sleazy.
His trip was seen as vaudeville blarney.
We spoke in Missouri at Neosho.
Truman saw the throng from the train's window

And was delighted. He spoke with gusto
For the seventeenth time that day. Something
Had changed in Truman's favor. Getting
These crowds meant we had a chance of winning.

We decided to save Ohio
For another trip, as well as Chicago,
So we stopped in Southern Illinois

And took a motor cavalcade driving
One hundred forty miles to the mining
Towns seeing large crowds yelling and cheering.

Democrats made post war reconversion
A success, avoiding a recession
With new jobs and a higher civilization.

Our VP candidate Alban Barkley
Helped us draw large crowds in Kentucky.
Then Truman spoke in Blue Grass Country:
No matter which horse leads during a race,
Or if the horse runs a fast or slow pace,
The first one to cross the wire wins first place.

In West Virginia on our last night
At eleven o'clock in the torchlight,

He spoke to an enormous crowd, a sight
That gave us goose bumps. The photographers
Turned their cameras on the crowd. Pictures

Appeared soon in major newspapers.

Early on voting day, take the ballot.
Cast your vote for the straight Democratic
Slate. You will be voting for your wallet.

After we chugged back into Washington,
He spoke to a crowd at Union Station.
He said he was in such good condition
That he would leave soon for Indiana,
Then Ohio, Illinois, Minnesota,
Wisconsin, New York, and Pennsylvania.

Pundits continued to believe that Dewey
Would obliterate Truman easily.
They developed a stream of nasty
Stories, casting him as an imposter,
Calling him a failed haberdasher
Who became a Presidential failure.
They wrote stories on Dewey's election,
Explaining how Dewey would lead the nation
And take over in the interregnum.

But Truman knew he had won the heartland.
He had been seen by over a million
Voters in thirty-three days. He was certain,
Although he trailed in the opinion
Polls, when the voters made their selection
Harry Truman would win the election.

Truman renewed his rolling campaign,
Seeking voters from the back of his train.
After the election, he would return again.
We said our good-byes at Union Station,
Listening to groans of the Magellan,
And waving farewell to Harry Truman.

* * * *

DWIGHT DAVID EISENHOWER
President 1957-1961

James Recalls His Limited Service to Eisenhower

As President, Eisenhower maintained
Distance between his office and staff.
He saw to it that we had been trained
To be crisp and efficient in our service
And to be attentive but act constrained
In our work when we were in his presence.

His eight years were a time of prosperity.
Eisenhower led desegregation
Of public schools and the military,
And forced Southern states' compliance
With an enlightened domestic policy
That advanced the cause of Civil Rights.

I did not do much for the President.
Occasionally, I would shag golf balls
For him, but it was on an infrequent
Schedule. Once he asked me for advice,
And I gave him a tip from a recent
Magazine I had removed from his office.

Lyndon Johnson was a frequent visitor.
It was known that he was a powerful
Man, and as Senate Majority Leader,
He could get things done without bothering

Eisenhower or ruffling feathers
On Capitol Hill or in the White House.

He asked me to keep my ears open
For relevant news and background gossip.
He called me his man behind the curtain,
And I willingly supplied him with
Reams of juicy background information.
He was generous in his thanks to me.

After Eisenhower left Washington,
He vacationed at the Annenberg
Estate. Having succeeded Kennedy, Johnson
Sent me there to help out the service staff
And obtain secret, useful information
Regarding news of an Alaskan Oil field.

* * * *

Eisenhower.
General Eisenhower ram rod straight.

JOHN KERR

Ode to the Classes of 1915 and 1965

Men of the Class of 1915, we salute you.
You have done your duty.
You are loyal and true.
You served your country
With courageous strength
And fearless bravery.
You fulfilled the oath
You made to the Army.
Some followed Fortune
Into the Infantry.
Cheer these men of action
With the roar of cannon.

Men of the Class of 1965, we salute you.
Spend your time preparing.
Only a very few
Can see what is coming.
Now the trees are taller.
The band is still playing.
We can still remember
Football games-leaves of gold
And red, Autumn's yellow
Challenge to make you bold.
Cheer these men who follow
Us onto War's tableau.

✯ ✯ ✯ ✯

Nixon

He never was much of an officer.
He never learned the Art of Command.
His only success was playing poker.
When he claimed that he had first hand
Knowledge of how my administration
Made policy, I sent the word to him
If he continued, I would take action
And tell my staff he was not welcome
At the White House. His vile, salty language
Struck everyone as offensive.

Said behind my back, it was an outrage.
From now on, I will be less supportive.
He is a rudderless politician
Who would be a bad choice for our nation.

* * * *

Mentors

For a career officer, a mentor
Is necessary in the infantry.
A junior officer needs to tether
Himself to one who understands Army
Life to obtain choice assignments.
Connor, Pershing and MacArthur gave me
The gifts of invaluable guidance
In exchange for hard work and loyalty.
I saw MacArthur create the image
Of himself as a skillful commander.
He worked hard to convey that message.
He was more an actor than a soldier.
A strong image was his greatest virtue.
In time, he became a living statue.

* * * *

End Play

The cottage is cold tonight. Wind and rain
Are back with us. Overhead an airplane
Drones toward London. A smoldering fire
Offers no warmth. Should anyone require
Coffee or snacks, my task is understood:
Care for the guests and maintain dry firewood.
I receive messages, empty ashtrays,
And for a while, I hold the War at bay.

A steady rain beats against the cottage
Door. The guests have been playing contract bridge
For hours. Our guests are Generals Bradley
And Gruenther. Ike and Kay Summersby
Are partners tonight. They have been playing

Well. They are bidding most hands and making
Their bids, so Ike is in a better mood.
I make fresh coffee and new plates of food.

We sit in silence, except for ticking
Of the hall clock. Sounds of card shuffling,
Dealing and bidding temporarily
Insert themselves into the reverie
Of the room. A pungent blue haze of smoke
From cigarettes and the wood fire evoke
A dreamlike feeling. Smells of fresh coffee
Rejuvenate layers of memory.

Absentmindedly, I began to pull out
Face cards from an extra deck and lay out
The Royal Families in an order
That might provide me with an answer
On how to stop the unfounded rumors
Being spread by a virus of whispers.

My first turned face card is the heart Queen
Who was the second wife of England's King
Henry the eighth, or so the legend goes.
I wonder if Mrs. Summersby knows
The extent of the malicious gossip
Being circulated throughout Europe.

If Anne Boelyn was the model sweetheart,
Should we then consider the King of Hearts
As our warrior king. He is the Supreme
Commander in Europe, held in highest esteem.
This King is different than the others.
In portraits, they appear as army brothers
Holding weapons. Our King carries a sword.
He directs it dangerously toward
His unprotected brain from his left side .
Does he know professional suicide
Will be his fate if he selects this Queen
And thrusts her into the Washington scene.

The King of Diamonds stands in profile,
As if he disapproves of this lifestyle.

With the Jack of Spades who holds the hourglass,
They see the time ahead when this will pass.
Neither are trustworthy. Both are one eyed,
Driven by army ambition and pride.

I continue matching cards with people
Who have contact with this command circle.
I see the Knave Club as Montgomery
Opposed to the Heart Jack Bradley.
Here are Churchill, Roosevelt and DeGaulle
Playing face card roles that are large or small,
Pending the war's outcome. Armies parade
As suits of Clubs, Diamonds, Hearts and Spades
To a Susa march. Brass, drums, and cymbals
Play stirring airs. The suits become symbols
Of power, privilege and hierarchy
Useful for post war titles and trophies.
We live in a world of raw ambition
In a milieu of misinformation.
Each decision comes with a second guess,
Then a blatant political finesse.

Our bridge games will end in less than a year.
Marshall will tell Ike where he goes from here.

* * * *

Finessing the Queen

Please come in. We are glad you could join our
Little group this afternoon. This is the hour
We gather three times a week to pass on
Rumors and gossip. Some are right, most wrong.
Each week we play many hands of Bridge.
It is a substitute game for marriage.

Earlier today we read a letter
From Colonel Butcher whose Bridge is better
Now that he and Ike have a little free
Time at the cottage for a quick rubber. He
Says Ike insists they always be partners

And play aggressively, taking no prisoners.

We are four army Queens, separated
From our Warrior Kings. Insulated
From privations that most women endure.
During wartime, we have found that liquor
And Contract Bridge push back the loneliness
That engulfs us. It fills an emptiness
In us. Contract Bridge is a metaphor
For life. We expect less from life, not more.

We live between boundaries of rules,
Conventions and protocols. Barrack schools
Have taught us the way we are to live when
Army husbands abandon their women
To pursue their military careers.
All of our men have been gone for three years.

Rumors persist that Ike's staff is aware
He is having a romantic affair
With a woman who is his staff driver.
It seems beneath him. A chauffer-lover
Has become grist for Hostess Washington
Busy bodies. At each party, we listen
To fanciful tales of indiscretions
By officers stationed near London.

This is not the first time that she has heard
Whispers about Ike. Her marriage has endured
Because of her will and tenacity
And Ike's need to maintain stability.

So we play bridge in our world, suspended
In time until this terrible war has ended
And all are home. Chimes from the grandfather
Clock announces we are an hour closer.

Oh my, please forgive me for prattling on.
I had no sense how fast the time had gone.
May I offer you cocktails or a snack,
Perhaps some port wine before you go back.
Did you put the dates on your calendar

For bridge with Mamie and Mrs. Butcher?

*Our bridge games will end in less than a year.
Marshall will tell us where we go from here.*

* * * *

*June 5, 1944. With officers and men waiting
to take off for the D-Day invasion.*

An Airfield Near London. June 5, 1945

In the distance, leaden rain clouds reach down
To a dark horizon. Paratroopers
And pilots stand at ease. There is no sound,
Except for a distant roll of thunder.

I pass through ranks of young men. I have heard
That as many as half of them will die
In the first hours of Overlord.
I smell rain and fear. We look at the sky.

Waiting. These brave men wait patiently
Near their planes for favorable weather
That will give us an Allied victory,
Or if it turns against us, a slaughter.

There are some lusty, rousing cheers.
It is difficult to look in their eyes.

If I do, I cannot hold back my tears.
So we all turn, and I look at the sky.

The invasion Armada is massed.
Now we need a favorable forecast.

* * * *

Unpacking for the Last Time

You were never home when it was time to move.
I was left alone to pack and remove
Those items to be sold or discarded.
Each time the news came we were transferred,
I had the feeling that all my dishes
Would be broken in a million pieces.
No matter our final destination,
I expected to see our possessions
Lost while in transit or manhandled
During unpacking and so damaged
They could no longer be useful to us.
Moving is part of military service.
Gettysburg is the end of that era
In our lives. I will unpack our china.
I will purchase some modern furniture
And uncrate my mother's sterling silver.
The farm is ideal, peaceful, and quiet.
This is our family's final billet.

* * * *

Recalling My Life

Your draft of the photograph album
Arrived last month from Washington,
And I have enjoyed looking
At the pictures and reading your notations. I
Sit more than I would like these days. My eye
Sight, which has been excellent, is failing.
So now, I am unable to do much reading.

Thank you for coming on such short notice.
As I told you in utmost confidence,
As my vision and hearing declined,
Strangely, my sense of smell improved.
It has become the primary sensory
Initiator of long-term memory.
Photographs of past events or news broadcasts
Trigger pungent aromas which can last
For days. I am washed in fragrances
Which cause me to relive experiences

Of early life, Mamie, our family,
The war, NATO, and the Presidency.
An early photograph you sent to me
Was when I worked at the Creamery
In Abilene. When I saw it, my nose
Filled with scents of milk and cream, rainbows
Of chilled foam, in the space and time
Of my past, an intuition of my mind.

Your album has produced a mixture
Of scents, but the smell of soaped leather
Has returned me to experience baseball
Games with my oiled glove, West Point football
On an Autumn day in leather helmets,
Fighting Navy in the final minutes.
My saddles in Panama and England
Had the pleasant smell of pungent almonds.

You may laugh, but the picture of my horse
In Panama brought out a ripe, coarse
And wonderful odor of fresh horse manure,
As complex a scent as a fine liqueur.
That long, forgotten fragrance returned
Me back to my days when I learned
Ancient history and the Art of War
From my mentor General Fox Connor.

Rank smells of mildew oozed from pictures
Taken in the wet Philippine summer.
Pictures of me in my dress uniforms
Became real as I smelled a rainstorm

JOHN KERR

Break the humidity for a short time,
Then resume cycles of mildew and slime.

Photographs from the war no longer
Could touch my spirit or capture
My feelings of perpetual worry
Until I smelled freshly brewed coffee
Wafting from the picture of my mess tent
In France. Its aroma gave pungent scents
Of chocolate, nutmeg, and hickory,
Foreshadowing an Allied victory.

Images of combat casualties
Struck me with the stench of blood and feces.
Rotting flesh, decay, and sour urine.
Odor held my nostrils in a prison
From which I could not escape. I was
Drawn into the photographs. In one, I pause
For a moment with young paratroopers.
The smell of death is on them. These soldiers
In hours will be lifeless carcasses
In France, abandoned in the darkness.

Then I looked at photos of the death
Camps. Reeling, I lost my sight and my breath.
Odors of human waste and acrid smoke
Invaded my senses and invoked
Horrible feelings of pain and despair,
Lives snuffed out by genocidal warfare.
It is one thing for life to be taken
In combat, but the murder of millions
Of people because of ethnicity
Is a war crime against humanity.

Pleasant scents and fragrances were brought out
By your later photographs which would spout
Aromas which drew me into the action
Of the photograph, whether it was bacon
Frying in France or a new deck of cards in
London or the pungency of stockyards.
Aided by my improved sense of smell
I broke free from my sensory cell.

I have relived my life, inhaling
Je Reviens perfume scents, exhaling
Mixed feelings of progress and beauty,
A new star and a new sense of duty.
Gasoline smells of a long motorcade
Blended scents with ticker tape parade.
When I acknowledged a welcoming roar,
Sour sweat wafted from the Convention floor.
Is anything as sweet as Spring in Augusta?
Freshly cut grass, dogwood and Azalea.

I am out of energy this evening.
Tomorrow we will do some more talking:
My New York years or the Presidency,
Or the current state of the Country.
We can address any topic you like.
I will tell you who thought up I Like Ike.

On your way out, look at our new painting.
General Robert E. Lee is standing
Below Pickett's Charge. That field is not far
From here. This shows the best of men at war.
I think. Notice Lee looking up the field.
If Pickett fails, then Lee's army must yield
And retreat. They played on a high wire
And fell. As you depart, please stoke the fire
For me. We may be in for some severe
Weather. It is cold for this time of year.

* * * *

JOHN F. KENNEDY
President 1961-1963

John F. Kennedy (signature)

James Speaks of John F. Kennedy

A New Generation Comes to Power

When Jack Kennedy became President
A new generation of Americans
Took up political life. The Silent
Generation gave way to flower children
And social activists. Civil rights
Became a national priority,
Which led to conflict between blacks and whites
And exposed the disparities
Of the two separate but unequal
Cultures of American life.
Suddenly, young people who had been tranquil
In the '50s were now creating strife,
Anxiety, unrest and upheaval
In the country. The Kennedys swept into
The White House ahead of this sea change,
But it was forming and would sweep through
America like a social tornado
Following Kennedy's assassination.

In the first days of his administration,
People were energized and pleased
With him. His wife entranced the nation
With her charm and beauty. She displayed
Talent in organizing receptions

And formal dinners for foreign guests.
Hers was the most coveted invitation
In the world, and she scrubbed the lists
To her personal satisfaction.

As requested, I continued observing
Daily comings and goings of interest
To Vice President Johnson, informing
Him of secret meetings and the choicest
Dark rumors which were circulating
At the time, most of which were unfounded
But always greatly appreciated.

What happened that November day
In Dallas will be in my mind forever.
Those memories will never go away.
There is a dark, empty void in the bottom
Of my soul which cannot be filled with poems.

* * * *

Sailing with Jackie.
Jack Kennedy points his boat into the wind off the Massachusetts coast line.

A Visitor from Cambridge

Welcome. Please excuse me for not standing,
But my condition has been worsening
Lately. I have kept it confidential
Thinking I would seem less presidential
And reduce my bargaining potential
If the true nature of my physical
Impairments and suffering became known.
For now, intense pain is my thorny crown

Which I wear daily when medicines
Prescribed by my Boston physicians
Fail to deaden or ameliorate
Stabbing, piercing pain that will not abate.

Please sit there on the couch. My rocking chair,
An ocean view, and the smell of sea air
Do much to restore my youthful vigor.
This place helps clear my mind for the rigors
Of endless congressional negotiation,
Which is inherent to my position.

Your drive down from Cambridge took longer
Today. Will coffee or something stronger
Refresh you? Perhaps wine or Cutty Sark?
We have plentiful stores of both in dark
Warehouses nearby, or so I am told,
Stored with deep secrecy by the old
Man during the years of prohibition.
Bootlegging whiskey made him a fortune.

You observe keenly. I have been reading
On ties between attitude and suffering.
There on the coffee table are classic
Works which deal with this important topic.
My books date from an Old Testament writing
To modern works on Positive Thinking.

I admire the optimism of Job,
But few have his strength. My faith would erode
Under the pressure of his afflictions,
Humiliations and degradations.

Classical tragedies produce an abundance
Of pain, but I still have my drug dependence
After reading through them. From Shakespeare's
Tragedies, I gained no solace. Poor Lear
Was so blind to his own problems, if you
Will forgive the bad pun, he scarcely knew

What to do. It was in Saint Paul's letters
That I began to see that my fetters

Would break if I changed my attitude
And accepted my frailties with gratitude.

He taught suffering leads to endurance,
And when character and perseverance
Follow, then the anger and frustrations
Which arise from difficult situations,
Recede, and allow hope and victory
Into life. St. Paul solved my quandary.
I used him to reshape my attitude.
Each day, I try to express gratitude
For the good things I have in life:
Parents, siblings, children and wife.

To the question of why we must suffer,
Or why someone's burden is heavier
Than another's, sometimes all we can do
Is wait in the hope that something new
Will free us from lives of pain and sorrow
And grant us a better life tomorrow.
For now, I will continue my medicines,
Treatments, shots, operations and braces
Until the day my hope is fulfilled
And a healthy life is regained.

I enjoyed your list of reading suggestions.
It contains imaginative selections,
Especially *Message to Garcia*.
Asking no questions, Roland helped free a
Captive people from Spain. Obedience,
Linked with personal perseverance,
Is an issue I would like to review
In some depth at my next meeting with you.
Please answer this question: Would Garcia
In today's world support us in Cuba?

The afternoon is fading into evening.
I apologize, but I am tiring
And need to conclude this conversation.
Later, we can resume our discussion
Over dinner, scheduled in an hour.
Look there, a fog bank covers the harbor.

I can smell a rainstorm heading our way,
Tomorrow should be a good day.

* * * *

Smoked Pork

From the next room, bursts of laughter
Mix with scents of freshly brewed coffee.
Hard work by Salinger and Schlessinger
Has created a happy family
From polar opposite political
Sides. Powers and O'Donnell found agreement
By using a hard-nosed practical
Approach for diffusing the arguments.
The room contains advisors and lawyers,
Consultants, legislative magicians,
Highly paid tea leaf readers, soothsayers,
Pollsters and elected politicians.

All enjoy smoked pork legislation,
Except the surprised pig and the nation.

* * * *

Pleasures above the Abyss

Standing at the edge of a precipice,
Or approaching the start of nuclear war,
I am washed in pleasant calmness,
Surrounded by intense hues and colors.
Absent are pains of mortal life
When I am snared in the jaws of chaos,
Or balanced on the edge of a knife.
I am alive when it is dangerous.
In private, the risk of discovery
Heightens pleasure, requiring concentration
To escape professional injury.
And feed my sensory addiction.

Pleasures are greater; colors are brighter.
In my dream, I am the high wire dancer.

Ready to Debate in Chicago.
Howard K. Smith, Moderator

Scant seconds until we launch the evening.
Presidential candidates debating
On live television with millions watching
Is a broadcast first. Nixon is sweating.
Kennedy sits there patiently, waiting
For me. I wonder what they are thinking.

Vice President Nixon

They said to look at the camera. Eyes
Steady. No eye movement. Stay focused
On the topic. Be a good guy. Surprise
Him by agreeing with that groomed
Rich boy who plays the rake worldwide.
During this debate, I will tan his hide.

This is not the first time we have grappled.
I will outflank him and hit him broadside.
He is all talk and will be handcuffed
By his answers when he is denied
Access to his aides. The television
Audience will see him dodge tough questions.

Ask who is in the ring and who sits ringside.
These can be great political lessons:
Who is engaged? Who sits untested?
Who has plunged into the boiling cauldron?
Who has the strength of flame-honed metal?
Not that verbal one who offers little useful.

I am going to complete my mission.
Tonight I will appear strong and noble,
Crowned as America's champion,
Revealed as wise and capable.
I am ready for this showdown tonight.
Bring on my opponent. Begin the fight.

Senator Kennedy

I was told my task is to appear wise
Beyond my years, relaxed, unruffled
And competent. I understand the prize
Will be lost by the one who has muffed
A question or appears self-satisfied.
Mr. Nixon and I are ready to collide.

On the campaign trail, I learned what is treasured
By the public. They want a sense of pride
When they cast a vote, not for a puffed
Windbag who speaks in clichés and bromides.
What they will see tonight is a Nixon
Trying to bluff, wet with perspiration.

I will use my *I Am Not Satisfied*
Speech, establishing a sharp distinction
Between Nixon and me. I will show wide
Differences exist in our visions
Of leadership. He is uncomfortable
With whom he is. Tonight he looks dreadful.

Poor Nixon. He is not paying attention
To the instructions. I must look peaceful
And certain I can fulfill the mission.
With his five o'clock shadow, a reptilian
Presence emerges in this half-light.
Nixon will lose this electoral fight

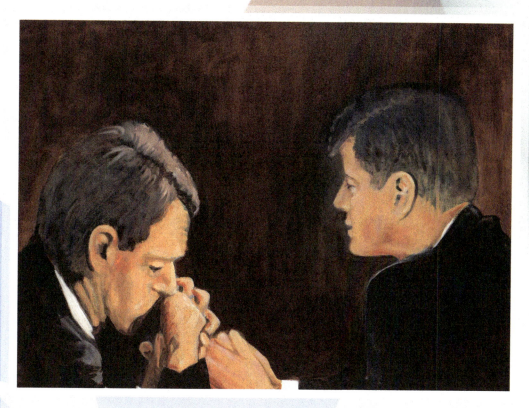

Robert and John F. Kennedy.

Joe Jr.

Alive, you dominated us. Your shadow
Slowed down time and everything we
Tried to do. We were a mere sideshow.
You were the brilliant star, burning brightly.
You won the prize for Academics.
While I fought to defeat my illness,
You excelled in campus athletics.
I fell behind in physical fitness.
Early, you taught me never to complain
And be prepared to do my duty,
Never to let anyone see my pain
As we advance our Church and Family.

We have an unquenchable thirst to win.
I keep thinking about what might have been.

* * * *

My New Attorney General

I have never known anyone so fearless;
I am transformed by your energy.
People whisper and say you are ruthless,
But our opponents lie in the debris
Of their failed, national election.
You are my true political hero,
Having used every tactical weapon
Against Humphrey, then Nixon. Is Castro
Your next target? I suggest the Teamsters
Will present a difficult obstacle
For us if you attack them as gangsters.
Consequences of that could prove fatal.

I must have the fig leaf of plausible
Denial when you start to fight evil.

* * * *

First Draft

I was most pleased with your suggestion
To employ a rhetorical question
As the architectural foundation
For my speech at the inauguration.
However, I have decided to use
An inverted form of that. Please excuse
My use of the starter "*Ask Not*" to fuse
A bond with those who share my views.

Why Not Ask Not

Ask Not, Rich Man, for a tax break. Your days
Of a free ride are over. Your taxes will rise
To levels more appropriate to the
Nation's long-term interest and purpose.

Easy money schemes are yesterday's
Headlines. Your greed has seen its last sunrise
Over Wall Street. A wave of nausea
Will choke you when you see what we propose.

Ask Not, Soldier, for an early discharge.
Rather, volunteer for Southeast Asia
Where you will be asked to sacrifice
Your life for a war few your age support.

A transfer and reassignment may recharge
Your career. It is better than Korea
In the winter. There is no snow or ice.
Say farewell. Soon it will be time to depart.

Ask Not, School Board President, for more time
To keep children of color from their place
In school. Reject Separate, But Equal.
Time for stalling and waiting is over.

What you have done is a Federal crime:
To deny these children because of race.
This black and white newsreel has no sequel.
School Master, relinquish your power.

Ask Not, Steel Maker, permission to raise prices.
Rather, show restraint and hold increases
Until the impact is less visible.
If you persist, you will feel our anger.

Instead, take a path that establishes
Low inflation growth which stabilizes
The nation and makes us a viable
Economic force, kept free from danger.

Ask Not, Union Leader
For our cover when you raid pension funds.
Ask Not, Foreign Leader
For gifts of grants and loans that never end.
Ask Not, Greedy Banker
For our blessing when you charge usurious rates.
Ask Not, Congressmen
For worthless pork to your Western States.
Ask Not, County Sheriff
For our help when you suppress the black man.
Ask Not, Southern Preacher, for forgiveness
When you sell hatred of your fellow man.
Ask Not, Teachers and Professors, for grants

When you do not lead the demonstrations
Ask Not, Farmers
For Soil Banks and crop eliminations.

* * * *

For Sorenson, the Nation's Son of Alliteration

Somewhere along the way, the rhetoric
Changed, and your speeches took on themes
Which challenged the heart and intellect
Of our audiences. You sang their dreams.
We learned to begin with humor,
Move to jabs at the opposition,
Use quotations from a famous author,
And finish with flurries of alliteration.
In the end, it came down to who I am
And the steps I take as preparation.
I will test my beliefs and where I stand,
As I prepare to lead the nation.

Through you, I pledge a fearless faithfulness,
A promise of ageless purpose and fairness.

* * * *

A Dangerous World

We live in a dangerous world.
Acting as international sheriff
We watch as freedom is imperiled
And wonder if our policies are tough
Enough. Should we continue containment
Goals and strategy in Southeast Asia

While boldly strengthening our commitment
To protect Western Europe from Russia,
Or should we focus on this hemisphere
And return to isolationism?
It would reduce the threat of nuclear
War and stem the tide of communism.

We must act in our long-term interests
With unmatched courage and firmness.

* * * *

The Window

Sunlight pierces floating dust and warms my
Face. Ancient links between hunter and prey
Are worshipped silently. You and I
Are joined forever, after today.
Rainbows of color dance from the window,
Refreshing the hunter on the mountain.
Pigeons coo greetings from the ledge below
To the herd approaching the canyon.
Steady. No rush. Time flows, then glides slowly.
My thoughts cease, I hear rhythmic breathing,
Now I am at peace, waiting patiently.
The herd arrives. I act without thinking.
My work is done. Feeling and sensation
Return. Now cunning replaces action.

* * * *

Kennedy with Nikita Khrushchev in 1961.

Parkland

Black cars skidding to a shuddering stop
Discharge a scene from gruesome hell. The top
Of one of the victims head is bloodied
From a massive wound. It is a ghastly
Sight. Around the entry and exit wounds
Purple coagulate is forming. Sounds
Of grief and anguish pierce our souls. We feel
Pressed by a great weight in a surreal
Prison. A sea of numbing confusion
Engulfs us, the toxic gift of a gunman
Who has escaped. Someone is shouting
For quiet, but no one is listening.

* * * *

An Unlocked Door

The door is unlocked and unguarded.
Inside, the man I knew as O. H. Lee
Is being held. I am isolated,
Trapped, helpless. Can anyone save me?
Soon after this began, I was called
By two connected people who said he
Was dangerous and should be neutralized.
Oh God, I am scared. I cannot flee.
On the third call, they stopped listening
To my frantic pleas to be removed
As the fall guy in assassinating
Lee before he strikes a deal with the Feds.
Now he walks toward me with his guardsmen.
In his eyes, there is a flicker of recognition.

* * * *

LYNDON B. JOHNSON
President 1963-1969

Introduction: James Recounts His Days with Lyndon Johnson

I have been speaking on this stage too long,
And you have shown patience for my songs
Of Herbert Hoover through John Kennedy
Who put Johnson in the Vice Presidency,
Thinking he would be marginalized
And shoved aside. He was despised
By the Kennedys. Some had objected
To his being on the ticket, preferring
Almost anyone to Lyndon, but carrying
The south and west were the deciding
Factors in his ultimate selection,
And Kennedy carried the election.

I had a long relationship with Johnson
Which began in Truman's administration
When Lyndon was a Congressman
From South Texas and the leg man
For Sam Rayburn who was the House Speaker.
I had a side agreement with Lyndon:
I would keep my eyes and ears open

For important unknown information
Which might strengthen Johnson's rise to power.
In this town of innuendo and rumor,
I fed him a regular diet of certain

Congressional social indiscretions:
Associations with persons of ill repute,
Entanglements headed toward lawsuits,
Shady business dealings and connections,
Party stalwarts conspiring against him,
Or pork barrel Congressmen out on a limb.
Most of these were less fact than fiction,
But he seemed to enjoy them. I never
Was discovered. I was his secret partner.

When Lyndon left the White House, I followed.
He gave me a job at the Ranch which allowed
Me to reflect on my forty-one years
Of service. As my life winds down and nears
Its conclusion, I find I have much to be
Thankful for. Serving leaders of our country
Up close gave me the opportunity
To study six presidents in action,
And how they dealt with unbearable tension.

The conflict I remember most vividly
Was early in the term of John Kennedy.
In the '60s, the Soviet Union challenged
Us with long-range missiles in Cuba aimed
At our East Coast. Our leaders were tested,
And a nuclear war was averted.

One of my favorite poems is "Sunset"
Written in his final days. The setting
Is the Perdernales in near darkness.
All that Lyndon did will soon be ashes.

* * * *

Johnson takes the oath of office on Air Force One *in Dallas.*

Resigned to his fate.
Johnson reaches the decision to not seek an additional term as president. The press is unyielding in their opposition to him, the war in Vietnam continues and is unpopular, and the country is polarized.

Coffee at the Driskell

So there you are. Sorry to be late,
But a car wreck added an hour's wait.
I was not sure where to meet you, but the
Front desk said you were here having coffee.

How long has it been? It was the panel
For PBS, which led them to cancel
The series, I believe. Try a kolachi.
I think they come from a German bakery
Near Austin, and they are exceptional.
Try the apricot. They are delightful.

This morning I thought about our session
Today, and I assume your position
On Johnson's legacy remains unchanged,
Or perhaps it has been strengthened.
I have developed new sources who confirm
My research. My opinions remain firm.

After the panel, I would like to buy
You lunch at Stubbs. Their brisket makes you sigh
It is so good. After lunch we will drive
To San Marcos. I plan to arrive
Late afternoon, assuming I-35
Cooperates with us and no Nafta
Eighteen wheeler truck scrimmage puts a flaw
In our plans. Tomorrow you have lectures
In the morning, followed by a seminar.
I will return you to the Driskell Hotel
Where we will say our final farewells,
Assuming we are still speaking
After appearing together in five meetings.

Let me begin by saying how much I
Appreciate your support, but seeing eye
To eye with you on any politician
Much less a figure like Lyndon Johnson
Is impossible to reconcile.
Our disagreements over substance and style
Are well-known. You are committed to what

Happened, so your research stops at the casket.
You judge Presidents contemporaneously,
While I focus on Presidential legacy.
I seek to know which accomplishments
Transcend decades and continue to the present.

Well, I think your characterization
Of my approach and research positions
Could be a little more generous,
But you become the consummate actress
When you lecture on the lasting impact
Of some long ago, forgotten contract,
By dragging it up from history's basement,
And somehow making it seem relevant.

We have an hour before we need to leave
For the Johnson Library. Your lecture, I believe,
Marks your first formal, public assessment
Of his legacy. You have been silent
For thirty years, so if you will share some
Of your findings before we reach the Forum,
I will have another cup of coffee
And satisfy my curiosity.

I agree. What I am going to say
Will disappoint you. LBJ
Should be measured by what he produced,
And his reputation should be rescued.
He changed the nation's social landscape
Only second to FDR's reshaping
Of the American economy.
Never has any president so boldly
Acted to bring about social justice.
He was at the forefront of a bloodless
Civil War to eliminate poverty
And grant civil rights to minorities.
He recognized that incremental
Legislative solutions would curtail
What was needed. He thought he could prevail
On a broad front. His Great Society
Was the declared legal war on poverty,
Civil injustice, poor education,

Lack of good healthcare, bad transportation,
Inadequate economic opportunity
And the weaknesses of Social Security.
This is the main thrust of my presentation.
I can give a more detailed explanation
Of each of these legislative
Actions, if you would like. Initiatives,
Such as these required a superhuman
Set of skills, embedded in this Texan.
His legacy deserves better from this nation.
We owe him lasting adoration.

Perhaps you are correct, and I have over
Stated my viewpoint. His speech at Ann Arbor
Launched the plan for socialization
Of most aspects of life in the nation.
As we have time before we depart,
I will speak on his legacy. A part
Of me agrees with you, but the division
He created with his indecision
On whether to escalate the war in
Vietnam started an open rebellion.
It united more than half the people
Against him. He was caught on an anvil
Built by the military who said victory
Was probable and hammered by angry
Young people, academics and the press.
It was a time of violence and unrest.
It was the first use of television
From a war zone, bringing revulsion
Of the public who watched in horror
Each evening, forced to watch the war.
The Vietnam War was his albatross.
His legislative triumphs have been lost.

Yes, that summation of the war is true,
But his legacy, I will argue,
Lies in what he accomplished for poor
People, the elderly and those whom he swore
To protect when he took the oath of office.
I am able to look past his coarseness,
The war and his near-term public judgment

To sing a song of thanks that this talent
Could lead us in such a critical
Period. We should be eternally grateful.

I think it best that we bring this to an end,
And prepare to leave. We should suspend
Our discussions until we are safely
On the road to San Marcos. His legacy
Can wait for us a few days longer.
Who can say? The wait may make it stronger.

As we leave, please notice the collection
Of photographs taken here from election
Night parties during various campaigns.
You can almost smell the bourbon and champagne
Through the cigar smoke and hear the laughter
As Johnson's winning margin grows larger.

****

Meeting President Roosevelt

President Roosevelt, Welcome to Galveston.
Was fishing in the Gulf of Mexico
To your liking? We heard you caught Tarpon
And Kingfish by the bushel. Do you know
Our freshman Congressman, Lyndon Johnson?
He ran on your platform, helping us grow
The Democratic Party's control in his district.
He ran his campaign on social reform,
Asking that the outcome be a verdict
On the Court, the New Deal and your platform.
We think young Johnson will be a perfect
Addition who will come in like a windstorm.
If you have time, sir, perhaps some photos
With Johnson, sent to his constituents
Will make you both bonded, Texas heroes.
Johnson seeks to meet you and is present.
Would you mind? That classic FDR pose
Is what we need to record this event.

****

Touring the Ranch

During cocktails we got in the white Lincoln
For a guided tour of the Ranch. Johnson
Drove, placing a paper cup of Pearl beer
Between his legs. He kept one hand free to steer
The car. The other rested on the thigh
Of one of his female assistants. My
First thoughts were overwhelming concerns
For us and for the trailing Volkswagen
Bus behind us, filled with journalists
A bartender, liquor, and lobbyists
From Houston. We drove through a dry creek bed,
Climbing out near the family homestead
Where we stopped. The bartender poured
Another round of drinks, and then we sped
Toward Johnson City for a brief tour.
We were back at the Ranch in an hour.

We loaded the bus with ice and shotguns
And standing in the sun roof made a run
Toward the cattle water tank looking
For skunks. Finding none, we began shooting
At anything that crossed our path.
A rusted tractor caught most of our wrath.
It never struck us as we were laughing
That men in Vietnam were wounded and dying.

* * * *

Lyndon Is for the Little Guy

Lyndon always stands for the little guy.
He knows what it is like to be on the
Short end of the stick, unable to buy
Enough food for his family or see
How he could ever earn enough to pay
Off his mortgage to the county banker.
All of you can still remember the day
He brought those folks down to hear the farmers.
And quick as a wink, we got some relief.
He got dams built and cleared cedar breaks

Which brought up springs of water for our beef.
And now with the REA, it takes
Us into the twentieth century.
We can listen to the radio or
Sew on a machine using electricity.
Because of him, I am not poor anymore.

* * * *

Campaigning

I have learned the hard way that winning
Elections requires nonstop campaigning
And an effective organization
That can deliver voter registration
And winning votes on Election Day
To defeat the opponent in a way
That he is unable to recount and find
More votes before he runs out of time.

Tonight we are campaigning in Waco.
My helicopter is part of the show.
Once we are in the arena, we will circle
The stands in an open convertible.
I will speak of my concern for the little guy,
Make fun of eastern hypocrites, and express my
Desire to be of important service
To the people of the State of Texas.

* * * *

Big Tex at the State Fair

Lyndon is driven to be the big man.
He enjoys knowing what it is to be
On the long end of the stick so he can
Drive competitors to ruin and then see
The least collateral needed to pay
For a business, using crooked bankers.
All of you recall that on the same day
Banks were foreclosing on working farmers
He got TV licenses in his wife's name

From a corrupt FCC for three stations.
Lyndon used the Fix, but he felt no shame
For using clout to swindle the nation.
He loved the electoral process,
Often asking voters long ago dead,
But now willing to assure his success,
To appear in alphabetical order when they voted.

Maybe he is Big Tex at the State Fair,
I saw him in Dallas at the OU game,
Standing fifty feet tall and full of hot air.
He looked sad when I called his name.

* * * *

A Bitter End

I never thought it would end this way,
People screaming Hey, hey, LBJ,
How many kids did you kill today?
They act as if I set out to betray
Americans and expand our foray
In Vietnam, using it as the gateway
For an assault on China, a doomsday
Forecast to heighten distrust so they
Can keep me from running again. I may
Announce that soon and then walk away.
Damn the Kennedys and the CIA
Who want me to walk out that doorway.

* * * *

Sunset

At sunset, the banks along the river
Lose their limestone color. Not a whisper
Of sound can be heard. The sun lurks below
The horizon, releasing an arrow
Of amber into the leaden, charcoal
Sky. Some say it is the sun's attempt to roll
Back the day which allows us time to clean
Up our mistakes. On the ocean, a green

Flash rolling back up to the horizon
Meant good luck and acted as a bailsman.

I am isolated on this island
Of charcoal grass: dying, ruined, shunned.
I sense this is my last sunset today:
Amber, green, and blue memories are gray.
In my mind, all I can see are faded
Colors and hues. My vision is shaded.
Large vases of yellow, Tyler roses
In the White House are buckets of ashes.

****

Johnson at his ranch in Texas, 1972.

The Old Man Speaks for the Last Time

Come close to the bed and sit beside me.
My eyesight has failed. I cannot see.
I will speak with you until my voice fails
And provide you with stories and tales
Of the six Presidents from Nixon,
Through Ford, Carter, Reagan, Bush and Clinton.
I was sixty-eight when James resigned
To follow Lyndon Johnson who decided
Not to seek reelection because he
Was so unpopular. The country

Was polarized over a foreign war
In Vietnam. Young men were dying.
The Selective Service Draft was causing
Great unrest, and vocal opposition
Challenged the leadership of Johnson.

His decision to not run shocked
Some of his supporters, but he walked
Away from Washington with great sadness
And took Lady Bird back to Texas.
Johnson, James and I lobbied Nixon
To replace James with John, James's son.
Nixon agreed, so John came to work for
The communication staff to help secure
Private exchanges of information
Between members of the administration.

My memory does not serve me well.
I cannot recall much after the hell
Of Nixon's pending impeachment,
Ford's pardon to avoid an indictment,
And Washington breathing much easier
After the election of Jimmy Carter.

I recall vividly that Reagan drove
Carter out after one term. Reagan wove
A tale for the American people
Of pure fantasy, an unbelievable
Movie script created by Hollywood
Which fabricated how he would
Pull America from its malaise,
Reduce government spending and outlays,
And cut taxes to restore the middle class.
The press, for the most part, gave him a pass.

Being President was the pinnacle
Of George Bush's career and the final
Stop on a long road of public service.
He served the office with a purpose
And should have won reelection easily,
But Bill Clinton campaigned tirelessly
And upset him. I never met anyone

Like Clinton. He was the man for all seasons.
With all his faults in view he could disarm
An angry critic with his wit and charm.

Now the attendants want me to conclude,
And I do not think I am in the mood
To anger them. This has been tiring
And my strength is weakening.
When my endurance improves, I will ask
You to return so we can complete this task.

* * * *

John Speaks of the Presidents His Family Served

All of us are getting older,
And this box I hold is no exception.
Inside it are aging files and folders
Containing stacks of poems written
By Presidents and collected
By three generations of our family
Who for a hundred years have served
Here during the twentieth century.

Robert, my grandfather began our tradition
And served a short time with McKinley
Until his tragic assassination
In Buffalo. It was a tragedy
That propelled Teddy Roosevelt
At a young age into the office.
McKinley's financial backers felt
Moving Roosevelt from Albany
To Vice President to be a safe play
And rid them of a trust buster,
But they came to regard that day
As the one when the Trusts lost power.

Roosevelt was followed by Taft
Who really wanted to be Chief Justice,
But he lacked skill at Statecraft,
And Roosevelt undercut him with a circus
Act of political feints and maneuvers

To form the Bull Moose third party
Which caused an electoral disaster
For the Republicans. Eventually
Taft was named Chief Justice
By Warren Harding who succeeded
Woodrow Wilson after he left office.
After World War I began Wilson led
Us into war during his second term,
Then afterward worked hard for the League
Of Nations, but Congress would not affirm
Support because of political intrigue.

From what I read, Warren Harding
Looked Presidential when he ran,
For President, but a good-looking
Man was not enough. His sidemen
Did him in with graft and thievery,
And he died while travelling out West,
Some said it was because he felt so guilty,
Others said it was the fear of arrest.

My grandfather followed Coolidge
Out the door when he retired.
Republican candidates back stage
Were kept waiting because Coolidge declined
To let anyone know if he would run
For office again until it was too late.
Grandfather decided his work was done,
And supported Hoover as the candidate.
Grandfather approached Hoover directly
And asked if my father could replace
Him in the White House. Immediately
Hoover agreed, so my father found space
Nearby. In '38 that was my birthplace.

* * * *

James Worked Forty-One Years in the White House

My father James worked for forty-one
Years here. He started with Herbert Hoover.
Then did everything he could to hold on

With the Roosevelts, starting as a chauffer
Then eventually as a trusted aide
And confidant for twelve years,
Reporting to Eleanor when Franklin strayed.
It was a dangerous game, but his fears
Never materialized. During this period,
James came into the circle of Lyndon
Johnson who, without question, cultivated
Him and used him to obtain information
On political rivals and opponents.
When Roosevelt died, Truman
Surprised us with good judgment
And the courage to make hard decisions.
Truman had a low opinion
Of General Eisenhower
Of whom he said that Ike
Was a better golfer than leader
And Truman found nothing to like.
After Eisenhower left office,
A bitter contest was won by Kennedy
Over Nixon bringing in persons
Of talent and achievement
In the arts and scientific accomplishment.
Kennedy treated Johnson poorly
Who did not like it and acted crudely.
Like the industrialists who made Roosevelt
Vice President and came to regret
It, the Kennedy brothers later felt
He was a mistake. Johnson was a threat
To them after Kennedy's assassination
Came down so hard on the nation.

★★★★

John's Farewell

Between dusk and night, a flare
From below the horizon
Sent magenta and flaxen hues
With streaks of lemon
Through the evening air,

modifying our view
Of the western sky.

It is time to say good-bye
To Nixon, Ford and Carter,
Close the book on demons,
Build houses for the poor
Bank the fires of passion,
Support finding a cure.

Say farewell to Ronald Reagan,
George Bush and William Clinton
Who write books on the future.
They speak like statesmen
Retreating into the shadows.
History is our new fiction.

The generosity of William Clinton
Secured me work in Little Rock
Where I will shuffle papers and talk
To anyone who will listen
Until someone drops the final curtain.

Darkness pushes the light away
At the end of an active day.

* * * *

RICHARD M. NIXON
President 1969-1974

Introduction: Nixon Was a Complicated Man

Nixon was a complicated man,
Bright, confidant but too paranoid.
His isolation was not healthy. Haldeman
And Erlickman formed a schizoid
Circle around him which kept
Fresh ideas and opposing views
From reaching him and swept
Out arguments which were breakthroughs
In innovative and original thinking.

Nixon was charged with ending the war
In Vietnam which he accomplished,
But it was increasingly unpopular,
And so was Nixon as the years continued.

His personal grasp of complex international
Issues was exceptional, and he relied
On Henry Kissinger for advice and counsel.
Working together, the two of them succeeded
In the relaxation of tensions with China.

For all he did in foreign affairs,
The public never liked him personally.
He seemed to wilt in the harsh glare.
Of television. He looked untrustworthy.

Arrogance and paranoia led to his downfall.
He and his staff lied about Watergate.
His Vice President was caught in a scandal.
To avoid prosecution, Nixon resigned in disgrace.

* * * *

Rice Paddy

Thump, thump, thump fades
Off to the West,
Where a pillar of smoke rises.
Rain has stopped,

No longer trying to clear the stench
Of rotting crops,
An eerie silence blankets
The grass around us.

Everyone is down on the ground.
Up ahead, someone saw movement
In the thicket, perhaps a sound,
Perhaps a glint.

Get up, move forward.
Fear clogs my throat.
It is hard to walk forward.

* * * *

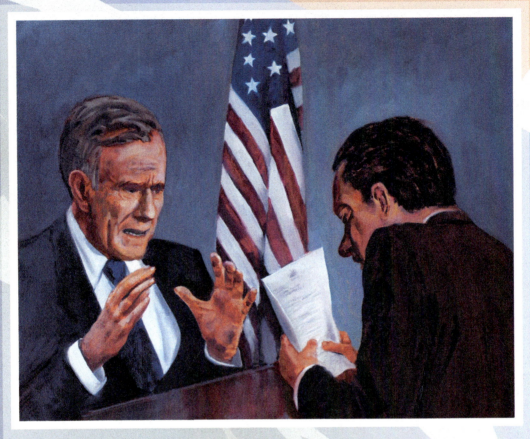

George Bush Confronts Nixon.
George Bush, as head of the Republican party during the Watergate era, confronts Nixon and demands that he resign for the good of the Party and the Nation.

Mentors

Nothing has ever been easy for me.
I never had a mentor who would see
Obstacles in my path and remove them,
Or pull me back from a shaky tree limb,
Show me how to fight an adversary
Or gain entrance to a fraternity.
I was rejected by Eisenhower,
Deemed unworthy by Rockefeller,
Summarily dismissed by Truman,
And embarrassed by Lyndon Johnson.
They viewed my role as Vice President
As a cosmic political accident.

Mind you, sir, I am not here to complain.
I am only attempting to explain
That I have always been an outsider
And never accepted as an insider.

* * * *

Despair

The piranhas are in the water.
I have lost again.
There is glee from the Press,
My own party and Democrats.
I cannot stay in California.
Where do I go from here?

* * * *

Touchdown

The crowd's roar washes over me
And bathes me in its joy.
Hit my spot.
Give them the grin.

Send them the touchdown signal
And the big victory V.
Flashing lights are everywhere.
Music surrounds me.

Give them another touchdown.
There go hats in the air.
Nothing is better than this.
Oh, what a sound.

* * * *

The Chameleon's Gyroscope

You have posed a difficult question.
You ask what is the internal compass

That guides me as a politician
And keeps me effective with the Congress.

Always, I know where the wind is blowing
And sense which bills will be rejected.
I can predict the results of voting.
I know who will not be reelected.
If I am pushed into a corner
And asked what is expected of me,
There is only one way I can answer:
I am whatever you want me to be.

In the predawn, do you ever shiver
When you first see yourself in the mirror?

★ ★ ★ ★

Real Politics

Please come in. Sit here. As my messenger
To the council, tell me what Kissinger
Is spreading around. Is he still training
Me daily? Is that what he is saying?
His deceit is written across his face
Every time he needs to be in this place.
He does have a good grasp of world problems
And effective ways to reduce tensions,
But if he cannot control his ego,
I will deep six him and let him go.
If he tries to take on this old fighter,
I will dump him on the steps of Hoover.

★ ★ ★ ★

A Cautionary Note

You have a new message from Goldwater
Who says that you are a natural fit
To unify the party. Your daughters
Want you to run again, but the pundits
Will treat you as the enemy this time.
In my mind, I do not think the nation
Is ready for another run. Your prime
Is past. Now what will be your mission?
Think hard on what they will do to destroy
You. Rethink this. Remember the nausea
And exhaustion? We have much to enjoy
Without going back into the arena.
You will always be my brave warrior.
I beg you, give us a better future.

* * * *

Agony

My bones are crumbling. Oppressive weight
Shatters me. Why have I become the villain
In this tragedy? My soul and heart break
Within my chest. Congressional hangmen
Will close the snare soon. I will be trapped,
Isolated and despised. No escape
Seems possible now for I am kidnapped.
I cannot breathe. I may suffocate.
Democrats demand my resignation.
I am their political prisoner.
Now my party deserts Richard Nixon.
It is unclear I can issue Orders.

Everywhere, I see the enemy
At work. I am dying of agony.

* * * *

GERALD FORD
President 1974-1977

Gerald R. Ford (signature)

Introduction: Between a Rock and a Hard Place

After Vice President Agnew resigned,
It took Richard Nixon a while to find
A replacement. When Nixon offered
The job to Ford, they had a strained
Conversation, but in the end he accepted
Richard Nixon's offer and was sworn in.

Ford found himself in a difficult position.
As evidence of the Watergate break in
Began to grow. He defended Nixon,
Against strong and vocal opposition,
But Nixon and his staff became frozen
As support for him began to weaken,
Leading to his forced resignation.

After Nixon left town, rancor and anger
Grew, with calls for a Special Prosecutor
To investigate Nixon and the Plumbers.
Ford was aware of the ill will and clamor
And looked for ways to bring closure
To the affair and focus on the future.

He felt there was only one solution
And that was to grant Richard Nixon
A full pardon, so on television
He announced his final decision.

Some said that it was a grand bargain.
Made earlier between Ford and Nixon,
The pardon cost Ford the next election.

* * * *

My Reason to Pardon Nixon Now

Should I deal with Richard Nixon's pardon
And end quickly this national nightmare,
Or should I give my administration
Some time? If I delay, it will impair
Me. We will be seen as a caretakers
In a decade of polarization.
Richard Nixon and I are prisoners.
He disgraced his office to the nation.
By allowing Nixon leniency
I can free myself to be President.
Extending an offer of clemency
Makes me the White House resident.
I know there is risk in this decision,
But it allows me to govern the nation.

* * * *

A Defining Moment: *President Nixon offers Ford the Vice Presidency.*

Stagflation

We have the worst of high unemployment
Now combined with rising inflation.
We lack legislative tools to confront
And best this economic stagflation.

I am torn apart by the newspapers
Because we cannot stop rising prices.
My business counselors and advisors
Have not shown me how to stop excesses
They say were caused by labor unions.
Big Business wants me to control wages
And tries to cast Labor as the villain.

Please take a good look at this WIN button.
Whip Inflation Now is my new slogan.

* * * *

Dealing with Assassination Plots

My security detail is warning
Of increased threats of an assassination
Attempt, but I have two public meetings.
And cancelling evades the question:
How should I act in a society
That is free? Use of the Secret Service
Is effective to assure safety
Of senior staff and make them less anxious.
I have no guarantees of protection
From an individual with a hand gun
Who is driven by an insane passion
To murder a senior politician.

The White House has lost two this century:
John Kennedy and William McKinley.

* * * *

Her Breast Cancer

Dealing with her breast cancer
Has been a frightful nightmare.
Countless cycles of x-rays
Have turned our joyous days
To endless consultations
And estimates by surgeons
On the probabilities
And their capabilities.
Where do we turn to contain
This modern plague of pain?

* * * *

Ford uses his pipe to buy time on a complex issue.

I Enjoy Smoking My Pipe

I enjoy smoking my pipe,
It is an activity I treasure.
In it I find a pleasure
Unavailable anywhere.
Smoking it restores me, wipes
Away the myriad cares
Of my job and energizes
And enables me to rise
And address the complex problems
Of the day and find solutions
That are best for the public,
Without regard to politics.

The joys of the pipe are earned.
A pipe smoker is a man in charge
Of his tribe or nation at large.
It keeps him thoughtful, unhurried,
Wise and capable of communion
With other time dimensions.

Often he is the shaman
Who leads a tribal nation,
Foretells where game is hidden,
When his people should plant,
When it is time to harvest
Whom they should believe,
Whom they should not trust.
He can interpret the stars,
Forecast a plan for war,
And unfold the mystery
Of achieving a victory
Over his adversaries.

Yes, I have used it as a prop.
It is a momentary stop,
Giving me time for reflection
Before I choose a course of action.
My favorite? A hard question
Perhaps this meerschaum,
Or that intricate, handsome briar
Made by a famous carver.
The best way to determine
Your favorite selection
Is to pick a tobacco,
A pipe, and give it a go.

Excellent choice. Cherry wood
Is hard, and its firm shape should
Promote cool temperatures
To let you enjoy full flavor.
My choice is this simple Clay
Which is one of the mainstays
Of my collection. Its basic.
Design makes it a classic.

I have several choices
Of tobacco, a few ounces
Of fragrant, aromatic blends.
Notice as the smoke ascends
Your heightened sense of smell
Will sense colors of pastel
Budding spring flower blossoms
And mature, late summer plums.
A wreath of gentle rising smoke
Will cause your brain to invoke
A rainbow of woodland smells.

After taking a draw, expel
A puff of sensory plume
Upward and into the room.
Sit back and relax with tastes
Of vanilla, embraced
By touches of caramel
Mixed with spice and apple.
Sometimes tasty ripe banana
Mixes with scented flora.
Beneath each complex layer
I taste hints of brown sugar.

You may find this tip helpful.
Always keep a bowl full
Of something new to try
At sunset with a glass of rye.

I enjoy as a special treat
Virginia, a subtlety sweet
Sensation on my pallet,
Not unlike roasted chestnuts.
Later you might consider
A tobacco pipe smokers
Love. Light brown, mahogany
In color. It is Burley
Mixed into many blends,
A tobacconist's best friend.

Then you should pursue English
Orientals, of which Turkish

Is best known. These exotics
Come with names that are classic:
Samsum, Izmir, and Cavella,
Or rare Yedidjes and Bursa.
Then try cured Latakia
And Perique from Louisiana.
And the complex Cavendish
Made by a special process.

So with that introduction,
Please take this special Balkan
As a gift to commemorate
What you learned on this date.
On your subsequent visits,
We'll discuss tobacco cuts:
Ribbons, cubs and curly,
Flake, shag and navy.

Let me escort you to the door.
Here, please look at my humidors.
Some are gifts from heads of state
This one from a college classmate.
My favorite is one in burl
Inlaid with Mother of Pearl.
My own personal favorite
Looks like a peach basket
Used for Michigan peaches
Carved by an artistic genius.

* * * *

JIMMY CARTER
President 1977-1981

Introduction: In Defense of President Carter

In the letter which accompanied
This draft manuscript, you have guaranteed
That anything said in conversation
Between us will never receive mention
In any of your works in the future
On the presidency of Jimmy Carter.
That being said, I will make my comments
To you, using counter arguments
To what I submit are false conclusions
And poorly developed opinions.
May I offer a glass of sweet mint tea
Before we start? This blend is one Jimmy
Enjoys and includes some Georgia peaches.
It cools the body and soothes the senses.
I grew the mint myself. It is spearmint
Which smells so distinctively pungent.
By the way, we hope you are able
To stay for lunch. Today our noon table
Will include peach iced cream and Vidalia
Onions fried in lard and a beef fillet.
So let us begin today's discussion
With a brief personal presentation
On how I view Carter's presidency
And his place in American history.
May I state what I think is your thesis:
He governed from a stance of weakness,

*And his views were of such naiveté
That his programs were in constant disarray.
Now let me take the time to present
An opposite viewpoint. In summary:
Carter was dealt many bad hands, and he
Did an exceptional job of reacting
To difficult situations, knowing
Solving problems from his predecessors
Would delay his programs for prior failures.
He inherited a looming crises
In energy which required policies,
Which if they were to be most effective,
Would force the American public to give
Up their wasteful uses of energy.
He made conservation a person's duty.
He asked us to drive and consume less.
For this, he was lampooned by the press,
And we were in no mood for sacrifice
Or willing to listen to his advice.
Looking back from a thirty year perspective,
We would be better today if we lived
Less dependent on Middle Eastern oil
And apart from that political turmoil.
He was successful in establishing
An energy policy, including
Conservation and new technology
For an unappreciative country.
To my way of thinking this summarizes
His tenure: poker with pre-dealt deuces.
You made much of his inability
To free hostages from our embassy
In Iran or deal with the Soviets,
But I say his actions left no regrets
When again viewed from a two-decade
Point of view. His actions were portrayed
As hesitant and weak. Look at Iran
Today, and Iraq and Afghanistan.
Do you think subsequent presidents
Have provided more effective guidance?
You have given insufficient credit
To what he did and have swept beneath the carpet
A long list of important achievements.*

He continued work on the Camp David
Accords reducing tensions and hatred,
Returned the Panama Canal Zone
To Panama which enabled him to set the tone
For new relations with Central America
And enter into a more rational era.
The Strategic Arms Limitation councils
Set the stage for reducing deadly missiles
And lessening the threat of a nuclear war.
Stagflation persisted during his tenure,
An economic hangover present
From Ford kept businesses stagnant.
Stagflation did play out eventually,
To the relief of the business community
In time for Reagan to take credit
For Carter's reductions in the budget.
My conclusion is Carter performed
As well as anyone could have expected.
Now please hold your comments
Until I have completed my arguments.
I will grant you that he left unpopular
With the public, facing an uncertain future,
But his dismal poll ratings were
Created by attacks from the Actor
And by the political ambitions
Of Kennedy's backers who bludgeoned
Carter on each issue relentlessly
To promote their candidate Ted Kennedy.

POEMS AND SONGS OF THE PRESIDENTS OF THE 20TH CENTURY

Confident.
Jimmy Carter is a picture of determined confidence.

It is my hope that you reassess
His achievements while he was in office.
I welcome corrections and challenges
From you, but I see they have set our places
For lunch. We can continue this discussion
Between the first course of fried chicken
And the fillets. By chance, did you notice
The nuclear submarine in my office?
That model was a gift from Rickover
Who was Carter's model of a leader.

✶ ✶ ✶ ✶

A South Georgia Evening

In my travels across America
Listening to working men and women,
I never saw a place like South Georgia
With its churches and schools for children.
There is a stronger pulse in large cities,
And lives move at a quicker pace,
But we live with limitless boundaries,
Beneficiaries of endless grace.
At night we sit in reverent silence,
Attempting to fathom our life's purpose
When the Milky Way displays its brilliance
As the evening sky unfolds above us.
Guide me to vocations of service,
A life devoted to peace and justice.

* * * *

When Hell Reached for Heaven

Angry with God's Creation,
Demons sprung from Revelation,
Destroyed Mt. St. Helens
When Hell reached for Heaven.
The mountain had been heaving,
The ground beneath was shaking.
Some of my friends vanished,
The day Hell reached for Heaven.

In the flame rode four Horsemen,
Fiends roaring in the cauldron.
I saw devils in the smoke,
Demons sprung from Revelation.

Day ended. We lost the Light.
Sleepless through a horrific Night.
Satan took his deadly time
Destroying Mt. St. Helen.

Forests were obliterated;
Streams and Rivers destroyed,
Works of a malicious Satan,
Angry with God's creation.

Animals were seized by Death
And buried by tons of earth.
Under a blanket of ash,
Nothing lived, complete destruction.

In the light of predawn
We can see one side is gone.
We see no living creatures,
Nothing but devastation.
Satan's try to reach Heaven
Destroyed Mt. St. Helen.
Nothing lives, complete destruction,
Nothing but devastation.

* * * *

Saturday Brunch Listening to the Football Game

The Georgia Bull Dogs play this Saturday,
So we will listen to the radio
To hear broadcasters call the play by play
And help us follow our football heroes.
During these games, we eat a lavish brunch
Of foods made from our peanut recipes.
For luck, each dish includes our local crunch.
Dips of ground peanuts, onion and cheese
Molded into the shapes of little
Footballs with pepper laces are starters.
We enjoy peanut cookies and brittle
After peanut soup and chicken tacos.
Sometimes Uncle makes a Jamaican Punch
From peanuts and some Irish Moss for lunch.

* * * *

Babe Ruth and Hank Aaron in Their Prime

Babe Ruth's record for major league home runs,
Which stood at seven hundred fourteen,
Was broken by the Brave's Henry Aaron
When he hit seven hundred fifteen.
We were guests in the box of Ted Turner
With Paul Erdos, the mathematician,
Behind Rosalyn and Jimmy Carter
And Dave Forney, a baseball statistician.
Carter thought he had Paul Erdos's number.
Jimmy said the records summed backward
Would be a prime of Aaron's and Ruth's homers
And it could work both sideways and forward.

Ruth's record, seven hundred fourteen, times
Aaron's record, seven hundred fifteen,
Yields the product of the first seven primes:
2x3x5x7x11x13x17x
Also, adding 714 to 715 yields 1,429.
Is 1,429 a number of baseball magic
In a set of primes like 1,249?
Was Jimmy onto a baseball secret?

The proof fell apart on what he could do
With the famous number 1,492.

* * * *

Hank Aaron Breaks Babe Ruth's Record.
Rosalynn Carter, Jimmy Carter, Paul Erdos, a famous mathematician, and David Forney, a statistician, join Ted Turner in his box for the game.

Extended Political Families

A politician needs a family
To support him on the long journey
To office, offering time and money
So he can be heard above his noisy
Opponents. I came home from the Navy,
Where I had worked for Rickenbacker,
And became a Georgia peanut farmer.
They pushed me to a seat in the legislature,
Then urged me to run for Governor.

When it came time to move up the ladder,
I consulted them all: brother, sister,
Wife, son, daughter, father and my mother.
I heard from my in laws and advisors,
Local preachers, sharecroppers and lawyers.
I listened to Atlanta bankers,

Received advice from total strangers.
I was stopped by a man on a tractor
Who suggested we pause for prayer
And solicit blessings from our Savior.
So when I decided to reach higher,
There was a large family of Carters
Who helped secure the office I desired.

* * * *

The Jimmy Carter at Rest in Kipsap, Washington

Lying quietly in the harbor,
Four hundred feet of submersible mischief
Is packed with instruments of terror
And machines to gather intelligence.
This Sea Wolf class sub takes thirty missiles
To sea. It uses clever, guided robots
To tap into underwater cables
Of the enemy and disrupt their plots
Against us. It can meet any test
By zealously following its motto:
"Simper Optima, Always the Best."
The entire crew adheres to that credo.
The deadly potential of the Jimmy Carter
Lies beneath the surface of the water.

* * * *

Early Fall on the Madison

Banks are awash in muted yellows.
Crunching along a shallow gravel bed,
We edge toward deeper water.
The strong current makes walking
Difficult, my boots fighting
Slippery rocks beneath me.
The roar of the river
Swallows all sound.
Time is suspended.

We pause to note
A new hatch whirling above us
In slanted sunlight
Of late afternoon sky.

Our guide points to a boulder
Dividing the rushing water
In midstream. In the
Eddy a large Brown
Awaits my presentation.
Twice my cast attracts no interest.
The caddis drifts away.

On her second cast, a fish strikes.
The reel screeches,
The rod jerks and bends.
The hook is set. Fish on.

I am here on the Madison
Fishing with Ted and Rosalyn.

* * * *

Frozen Images

Time moves quicker
Each passing year.
My eyesight grows dimmer,
And images are darker.
My knowledge grows deeper
As my insight gets better.

Here, look at this photograph.
(Does it make you want to laugh?)
It is a young man and his wife,
In the prime of their lives,
Walking down Pennsylvania Avenue.
Life is too good to be true.
He walks to his inauguration,
The elected leader of his nation.
For her, this is a pinnacle hour.
So strong, she holds equal power.

JOHN KERR

Images flicker back from time.
He waves, an analog mime,
A frozen man from other worlds
Soon to face tests yet unfurled.
He is a new type of leader.
He smiles at us; he is eager.

Look at this later picture.
He carries his own two-suitor.
The service said it was empty,
A stunt to portray Jimmy
As working man, who believes
He should roll up his sleeves
To make a point with that image:
Presidents shoulder the people's luggage.

He knew the use of symbols
Which often create national fables.
He will see his life as parables
When he sits to write his memoirs.

Take a moment to view this video
Of Sadat's funeral. Turn up the audio
If you like. Nixon, Ford and I are in flight,
And pose for pictures despite
Our feelings. We smile for the camera
And carefully avoid one another.
Please give me your impression.
Can you feel emotion and tension?

What do you think of these images
Of captured American hostages
Being humiliated and led around
Or tied to stakes, shackled and bound?
Are they symbols of failed policy?
By a nation grown weak and flabby?

Images dance through my mind.
Not all are so well defined:
Signing the accords,

POEMS AND SONGS OF THE PRESIDENTS OF THE 20TH CENTURY

Presenting awards,
Receiving the prize,
Crowds of enormous size,
Confronting the energy culture
With a cardigan sweater.
I think my place in history
Will be Habitat for Humanity.
By nailing two by fours
I improved lives of the urban poor.

My contributions to the future
Resides in works of the Carter Center.
Its impact will last beyond my life
And help reduce world hunger and strife.
I see you have stayed an extra hour,
So on our way back to the foyer
Please share your thoughts on this painting
Commemorating the Center's opening.
I think the painting may need cleaning.
Its once vibrant colors may be dimming.

Rosalynn Carter joins first ladies Nancy Reagan, Lady Bird Johnson, Hillary Clinton, Betty Ford, and Barbara Bush at the National Garden Gala in 1994.

RONALD REAGAN
President 1981-1989

Ronald kept a diary throughout his term.
My job was to keep his journals ready
For him at the end of the day. I read
His entries the next morning without
His knowing I was reading his journal.

John

Introduction: Dear Diary

Well, old friend we have been at this five years,
And we have shared the laughter and tears
Created by pressures of this office.
Foreign intrigues, domestic strife, Congress,
Visiting heads of state, ceremonial
Occasions, dealing with the press people
Are all part of what I am required
To do. I would be finished, exhausted,
If I stopped communicating with you.
Summarizing the day with a review
Of the highlights serves to energize me.
It provides me an escape valve and frees
Up my mind from the pressures of the day.
I can put my fears and concerns away
After I write down my thoughts and impressions
Of contemplated military actions.

Last month when I was at Camp David,
I reread four volumes of these and marveled
At the repetition of daily life:
Meeting with dignitaries and their wives,
Signing a piece of legislation or a bill,
In the Rose Garden with people pressing
Close to get into the picture, giving
A Ronald Reagan White House ballpoint pen
Or two for their wives, friends or grandchildren.
Events such as these make enjoyable
Written entries in this daily journal.

Other entries are difficult to write.
Nations seem eager to fight
One another over old boundaries,
So we and Russia arm them as our proxies
To avoid a direct confrontation
That would cause a complete annihilation
Of our countries. We are locked into
An arms race while looking for a breakthrough
In diplomatic negotiations
Which will restore peace between our nations.
We will win peace with a strong military.
Defending our safety is my sworn duty.

I have endless meetings with the NSC
Briefing me on threats against the country.

Central America is a target
Of the Communist party. Our Senate
Does not see this as a threat so they
Object and place obstacles in our way.
We must assist and support the Contras
Fighting the Leftists in Nicaragua.

My top priority is strengthening
My ties to Gorbachev. I am counting
On a strong personal relationship
Built by understanding and friendship
To see us to the end of the Cold War.
Such are my thoughts for this daily memoir.

On the home front we need to do better.
Lingering questions still need answers.
I can see the economy humming
If we could get Congress to cut spending,
Reduce personal and business tax rates,
And stop their endless class warfare debates.

Being President has many perquisites
Available, but the best, I must confess
Is *Air Force One*. At first, it was a luxury.
Now, I think it is a necessity.

I get a lump in my throat when I hear
Suza played by the Marine Band. Tears
Could not be held back when I saw a child
Crippled by disease, yet able to smile,
Waiting patiently to shake my hand
While listening to the Marine Corps band.

I thank you for your silent reflection
On these unvarnished communications
Because it is getting late, I must end
Our session until tomorrow, Your Friend.

****

Reagan at the Ranch.
Ronald Reagan enjoys the horse presented to him by the president of Mexico at his ranch, Rancho del Cielo, in California.

At the Movies

Hell Cats of the Navy
Brother Rat and Baby

Desperate Journey
This is the Army

Dark Victory
Sergeant Murphy

Swing Your Lady
Million Dollar Baby

John Loves Mary
Storm Warning

It's a Great Feeling
Smashing the Money Ring

Knute Rockne-All American
Girls on Probation

Code of the Secret Service
Naughty but Nice

The Cowboy from Brooklyn
Accidents Will Happen

Louisa
Cattle Queen of Montana

Juke Girl
That Hagen Girl

Boy Meets Girl
Law and Order

Tennessee Partner
Love is in the Air

Secret Service of the Air
Murder in the Air

Kings Row
Bedtime for Bonzo

Going Places
Angels Wash Their Faces

Tugboat Annie Sails Again
Hell's Kitchen

Campaigning with Five by Seven Cards

Mr. Chairman, your kind introduction
Again reminds me that big Government
Is the problem. It is not the solution.
A bloated bureaucracy will make us insolvent.

(Appear concerned)

This happened when I was Governor.
It is one of my favorite stories.
I was assailed by a State Senator,
In front of his lobbying groupies.

(Smile knowingly)

He said I had made a foolish proposal.
My plan to return our budget surplus
To the taxpayers was irresponsible
And revealed a financial weakness.

(Look incredulous)

Well my friends, for once I lost my temper.
I explained to him it was not his money!
He thought workingmen were tits on an udder,
Or beehives bursting with honey.

(Become indignant)

Get your hand out of the workingman's pocket.
You are nothing more than a pig at the trough.
I yelled at him: Let go of his wallet.
Leave him alone. Keep your greedy hands off.

(Enjoy the applause)

Then I said this to that Senator:
Take the word of an aging actor,
Stop your spend thrift boozing and get sober.
Remember you work for the taxpayer.

(Big smile—Step back—Wave)

* * * *

Commencement

Graduates: I salute you today
As you pass through this final gateway
To become the next generation
That leads our glorious nation.

I have some thoughts I would like to share,
Pieces of advice I heard somewhere.
It is my hope that in the future
You may recall one or two.

Be yourself
It is important to know who you are
And honor your parents and family.
Who created your personal history.
They show you the way as your guiding star.

Be thankful
Be thankful for your blessings,
Gifts of friendship, doctors and teachers,
A free nation guided by brave leaders.
Give deep thanks for the challenges life brings.

Be honest
Be known for truthfulness and veracity,
Playing by the rules, never cheating,
Known for never lying or stealing.
Never compromise your integrity.

Be optimistic
Work to find the best possible solution.
Focus on outcomes that are favorable.
Look for good in a man, not the evil.
Look for the cure instead of the symptom.

Be cheerful
Fill yourself with joy and encouragement.
Be known as one filled with happiness.
Share with others your cheerfulness.
To those in trouble, give peace and comfort.

Be persistent
To succeed you must exert perseverance.
Stand tall in the face of opposition.
Be strong. Hold to your course of action.
Take your time to reach your goal, show patience.

To conclude, I ask that you be cheerful,
And for all you receive, be thankful.
In your dark moments be optimistic.
Never forsake your goal; be persistent.
In every dealing, be forthright and honest.
Remember who you are, and be yourself.

* * * *

Détente

This meeting has been going on too long.
This group will do anything to prolong
It using words like glasnost and détente
As intellectual tripwires to taunt
Me. I have no use for diplomatic
Chess games to sustain academic
Egos who dwell on cold war counter moves,

As if their thoughts and speeches can improve
Our chances to reduce hostilities
And convince Russia to sign peace treaties
Which will be meaningful and long lasting.
I need to put an end to this babbling.
They argue for a delicate balance
With the Soviets with logical brilliance.
While I sit through their tedious lectures,
They line their nests with strategic feathers.
They live in a world of nuanced shadows,
Sensing mayhem from a hundred Castros.

They see the world through a cloudy prism.
Write this down to be put in my memoirs:
I will never allow a nuclear war.

Take care to note that when I interrupt
Them, their conversation will come to an abrupt
Halt, and each of them will be polite,
But each one thinks talking is his birthright.
No one wants to listen to what I say.
But I will stop their useless word play.

So, gentlemen, all this talk of Russia,
Contras, Cuba and Latin America
Reminds me of when I was a lifeguard,
With no specific plans for Hollywood . . .
Oh yes, I am told that lunch is served
On the east terrace and well deserved.
The meeting will reconvene at two.
Then I will complete my story for you.

* * * *

Assassination Attempts

My security detail is warning
Of increased threats of an assassination
Attempt soon, but I have two fundraising
Events. Cancelling evades the question:
How should I act in a society
That is free? Use of the Secret Service

Is effective to assure safety
Of senior staff and make them less anxious.
We have no guarantees of protection
From an individual with a handgun
Who is driven by an insane passion
To murder a senior politician.
The White House lost two in this century:
William McKinley and John F. Kennedy.

* * * *

Cargo

Shimmering heat all around us
Debilitating heat. Painful to move.
No relief. No escape from the baked earth.
We are in a furnace.
Fifty yards from the edge of the trees,
Heat so intense, animals are quiet.
No barking or yipping.
A din of insects calling
Presses on our ears.

Before we could shut down the engines,
We were hit by a wave of humidity.
Suffocating, we crawled from the cabin,
And stepped into a sea of misery.

Standing under the wing,
Seeking shade
From the heat and humidity.
Sweat pours from us,
Sits on my skin,
Cannot evaporate
Into clouds of humidity
Settled on this ancient riverbed.

Water from the canteen is warm.
Offers no help.
We flew in from Costa Rica.
Located the dirt airstrip

And set the DC 6 down.
Trucks rumbled up to the plane,
Unloaded cargo quickly,
Departed into the jungle,
Abandoning us to the insect roar.

We flew here from Costa Rica,
Located the strip held by the rebels,
Unloaded weapons for the Contras
In exchange for cocaine from the Cartels.

A small plane comes in low,
Circles and radios
For us to remain overnight.
There is an unexpected delay
New cargo will arrive at dawn.

Endure the night in the plane.
Put up mosquito netting
Over the cockpit window.
Dinner is a melted candy bar,
Lukewarm coffee and a cigarette.

At sunset, the heat is down.
Animals are out and howl
As they warn or kill
One another. Sounds of survival
And slaughter pierce the night.
Heavy insects assault
Netting on the cockpit window.

Here there is no border or boundary,
No system of compassion or ethics.
I live on stale cigarettes and coffee.
My home is the back of a DC 6.

At first light, two old trucks
Arrive, and we are loaded.
Heat and humidity follow
As we bump down the runway.
A new destination is ordered
For refueling and then a flight North.

Our refueling strip is in Mexico.
Then we will head North to Arizona
Where we will unload our secret cargo
Onto trucks bound for California.

* * * *

J. Peter Grace Reports to the President on the President's Private Sector Survey on Cost Control

Mr. President, how wonderful to see
You. I am here to report on
Your initiative to stem the out of control
Costs of running the Government. The goal
Of your Private Sector Survey on Cost
Control is to identify and toss
Out programs which are unnecessary
Or riddled with inefficiency.
You charged us to look for signs of waste
And when we find it to make sure we showcase
It. To help us find areas of abuse
Or evidence of purchasing miscues,
We recruited private sector executives.
We are ready to report our progress.
President Reagan, the situation
Is dire, and expense control is broken.
Every day we squander the future.
Congress is drunk on deficit liquor.
Unless we attack the waste of billions,
We will be in the hole for a trillion
Dollars by the fiscal year of 2000
Which equates to one hundred sixty thousand
For each heavily burdened tax payer
Whose neck is tied to a fiscal anchor.

We brought in one hundred executives
And placed them in thirty six task forces.
They came to us from the private sector
And began their work with zealous fervor.
With pride, here are their recommendations
Which are guidelines to restore the nation's
Fiscal footings and viability

And keep us financially robust and healthy.
Mr. President, we are ready to
Brief your senior advisors. I present
Key staff, Mr. Bolduc and Ms. Colson,
Our tour guides today on Cost Reduction.

* * * *

A Rainbow of Scents

Pleasant smells greet us as we awaken,
Sausage and eggs frying in iron skillets.
This must be the way it smells in heaven
Coffee perking, biscuits in the oven.

Work starts with horses in the morning.
In the barn we inhale the redolence
Of digested hay from pungent droppings.
Horses have their own distinctive fragrance.

Today we will spend the day on horseback,
So we repair the bridles and saddles
In a room that smells of blankets and tack.
Sweet, warm sensations infuse our nostrils.

This rainbow of scents: hay, sweat and leather
Inflame our senses with a spicy odor.

* * * *

Today's Horoscope
Aquarius (January 20–February 18)

Today is a milestone. Happy birthday!
Hone the skills you learned as an actor,
And follow your stars through the Milky Way.
Preside as our Great Communicator.
Repeat the great American story.
Use the gifts of modesty and laughter
To attain your place in history.
We strain to listen. You are our speaker.
Bend to hear advice from your spouse

Who is your best expert counsel.
She is your Gibraltar in the White House
And knows whom to trust among your people.

Astral signs warn of a White House scandal.
People you trust can ruin you. Be careful.

* * * *

My Lucky Stars

You have the chart in front of you.
Rhomboids, parallelograms held by circles
With twenty six triangles
Inside twelve divisions
Are frozen in time.

It is four sixteen
On a cold morning in 1911.
It is the sixth, an Aquarian Monday.
Someone has called for more water,
Or the baby must bear his own.
Hours, minutes and seconds
Are set, immutable.
Unless the time or birth is wrong,

Bring the tables forward,
Establish this native at the center of
The Celestial Sphere. Display
The plane of the equator and
Link it with the ecliptic.
Center the plane of the horizon.
Place the ascendant
Opposite the descendant.
Work through the Zodiac,
Lay out the signs and cusps.
There is much work to do.

Send out a celestial mechanic
To the highway of the Ecliptic
To mark the path of the newborn's journey
Using the Science of modern Astronomy.

Joan Quigley:

Astrology has many ancient forms.
In its early days, it was inseparable
From Astronomy. The Magi
Who sought the Christ Child

Were Eastern astrologers,
Following his star in the heavens.
Now Astrologers use new discoveries
To help interpret future events
And forecast possibilities.

If you doubt that we are influenced
By the stars, consider the effect
Of the Moon on ocean tides.
Like all the sciences, astrology
Evolves and makes advances
While defending itself from skeptics,
So-called authorities, enablers
Of the status quo.

We saw his Star ascending in the East
And followed it to your Kingly Priest.
From there we came to this lowly natal,
A night cave for keeping sheep, a stable.

Nancy Reagan:

I made a mess of things
Thinking I could keep my
Relationship with Joan a secret.
How naïve of me to be so trusting.
The White House is filled with people
Working their own agendas,
And they used me to strike
Against my husband.

It was inevitable that someone would
Betray me and belittle my desperate
Attempt to keep my husband safe.

After the assassination attempt,
I was consumed by fear that another
Attempt might be successful.
A friend suggested I talk with Joan
And see if I thought she might help me.

I felt a great burden was being lifted
From me as I spoke with her. She
Brought me great relief when she
Told me she could have kept the
Assassination attempt from happening
By looking at her charts and rescheduling
The events of that day.

It is a terrible thing to live in fear
When help is close in the Celestial Sphere.
The Stars can guide me and provide relief.
Such is my long held personal belief.

Don Regan:

The White House needed discipline
And a firm hand when I came over
To be chief of staff. I eliminated many
Communication lines to the office
And relieved the President from many
Worthless encounters and meetings.
He appreciated my organizational skills
Which gave him more free time.

Things went well, until Nance Reagan
Asserted herself into matters of state
For which she had no authority.
Under the influence of a clairvoyant
From California, she began to interfere with
Schedules, conducted conversations over
An unsecured phone and attempted
To set conferences and important meetings
Around what she called good days
And bad days for the President.

I was concerned that this Astrologer
Had too much control over the Reagans.
I was unsure of the extent she controlled
The President, but it was clear Mrs. Reagan
was under this woman's spell.
It was rumored that she had this woman
Cast a horoscope for Gorbachev before
The summit in Washington.

These antics would have been not much
More than mild distractions, except
There were serious problems in the
White House, not unlike the Nixon era.

Ronald and Nancy Reagan arrive in Los Angeles after leaving the White House in the 1990s.

Men who worked for the President
Were engaged in illegal activities.

They were selling arms to Iran
To finance an undeclared, secret war.

Basing policy on astronomy
Entwines the government with sorcery.
The fraud had nothing to do with Science.
They were purchasing cosmic insurance.

Don Regan:

The President thought his daily schedule
Was a script in which the main actors
Rehearsed and then acted out their scenes.
My job as chief of staff was to make
Sure that the President was ready for
His role for the day.

My service lasted only two years.
I was in full conflict with some of his
Advisors and his wife, and he
Had no spine with them. He was weak.

When it came time for a scapegoat
For the Iran-Contra, I volunteered
To play that role to spare the President.
As I was preparing to depart gracefully
He leaked my resignation.
I told him I deserved better.
I never spoke to him or his wife again.

The Friend preyed on a deep insecurity
While feasting on their vulnerability.
She was a twentieth century Rasputin
Who fouled the office of Ronald Reagan.

Nancy Reagan:

As soon as he arrived,
He began shaking things
Up in the White House,
Without being asked.
He forgot his duty

To the President,
He forgot for whom he
Worked, and he abused
Some very loyal supporters
Of the President.

He stiff-armed some
Congressmen and over played
His hand with many
People who had a need to meet
With the President.
He turned on me behind
My back, making me out
To be some Dragon Lady.
I would have fired him
Long before Ron got around
To asking him to leave.
Now he curries favor with the press
At my expense to sell his book.

On arrival, he was disrespectful.
On departure, he was disloyal.
He saw himself as the Prime Minister
Or Ronnie's Chief Operating Officer.

Joan Quigley:

I visited the White House only once,
But I was in constant communication
With Mrs. Reagan. We discussed
Many aspects of her life, and I
Provided what guidance I could
Based on my interpretations.
After the story came out
Regarding our relationship,
We terminated our work.
She was called hurtful names.
I know she was wounded by
The commotion and uproar
Over her reliance on Astrology.
I made a positive contribution.
I tell you that it worked.

Someone called me a cosmic waitress
Serving an aging neurotic actress.
This Science is more than parlor philosophy.
It is as old as human history.

* * * *

Evening at Rancho del Cielo

Sensations intensify at twilight.
Miles below, the sea turns black gray.
Orion stands guard in the early night
Above us. I am tired from a long day
Of hard, physical labor spent clearing
Brush this afternoon from
the east pasture.
Earlier, we cleaned the barn, enjoying
The sweet fragrance of
Arabian horse manure.
Rancho del Cielo lies in silence.
I sit at peace next to a mesquite fire
Seeking guidance and
relearning patience.
There is nothing material I desire.
A man should make an
effort to own land,
Clearing it and working it
with his own hand.

* * * *

Gentle Rain

The window is dark.
Autumn leaves rustle outside.
Time to arise, or

Time to go to bed?
I once knew that fellah who
Smiles at my breakfast.

Maybe it was he
Who put the glue and oatmeal
In my helpless brain.

A woman sits there.
Cannot recall who she is.
She is crying. Sad.

Smells from the kitchen
Conflict with cleaning supplies
And the Autumn rain.

I would like to live
Until the rain is warmer.
And the music ceases.

* * * *

GEORGE H. W. BUSH
President 1989-1993

John Sees a Sense of Purpose in Bush

I got to know George H. W. Bush when he
Ran the Republican National Committee.
Because he was the Committee's chairperson,
He could see that the damage done by Nixon
Over the Watergate controversy
Could destroy the Republican party.
He asked that I accompany
Him to a meeting with Richard Nixon
Where he would ask for his resignation.
He wanted a witness to his request,
A person who could later attest
To what had been said and verify
What was stated in Nixon's reply.
Bush showed a great deal of courage
To deliver that difficult message.

He believes that a sense of purpose
Should guide a person's public service,
And he has lived his life according
To that precept, never compromising
His belief in personal honesty
Nor his strict code of integrity.

Over the years I had interactions
With him, and he acted in the nation's
Best interest on every occasion.
I met him when he was a Congressman,

Then ambassador to the United Nations,
Delivered messages for him when he
Ran the Republican National Committee.
He left town as envoy to China,
Then returned to run the CIA,
Served as Reagan's Vice President,
Then elected in '89 as President.

* * * *

Because It Is the Right Thing to Do

Honor your ancestors' memories.
Embrace your extended families,
Because it is the right thing to do.

Be prepared to defend your county.
Then answer your call to duty,
Because it is the right thing to do.

Nourish and strengthen your family.
Teach them personal integrity,
Because it is the right thing to do.

Extend your hand to those less fortunate
Keep your charitable deeds private,
Because it is the right thing to do.

Let your guide to life be probity,
And conduct your affairs with modesty,
Because it is the right thing to do.

* * * *

George Bush ready to fly in the Pacific.

Back in Kennebunkport.
George Bush is back in port after an early morning cruise with his sons.

POEMS AND SONGS OF THE PRESIDENTS OF THE 20TH CENTURY

The Day They Brought Down the Chichi Jima Tower—A Ballad

It was the second of September in nineteen forty-four
When bombers were launched from an aircraft carrier
Stationed in the Pacific Ocean about an hour's

Flight from a key Japanese communications tower
On the Island of Chichi Jima. Four Hellcat fighters
From the San Jacinto joined with others
To aid and protect the four Avenger bombers
Whose job was to destroy the tower despite the dangers.

It was a day that lived on after the war.
The day they took out the Chichi Jima tower.

Hellcat fighters from the carrier Enterprise joined
Our assault force, but no enemy aircraft were expected
To challenge us that day. We had pounded
Their airstrip. We reached the target and commenced
Our attack. I saw the third bomber push
Into a wall of flame and flak, then rush
Toward the tower, with g forces crushing
Into the crew. The pilot was Lt. J. G. George Bush.

No one gave thoughts to the prospect of failure.
The day they brought down the Chichi Jima tower.

Early in the dive, the plane was hit. Smoke began pouring
From the starboard engine, and flames began shooting
Across the wing. On line to the target, Bush continued diving
Even though the plane was in danger of exploding.
At the target, his bombs, scored devastating hits
On the tower. I could see the flames from my cockpit.
The radio station could no longer be able to transmit
Our movements. We had blown it into twisted bits.

George Bush turned his burning plane toward the water.
The day they blew up the Chichi Jima tower.

He had to get his plane away from the Island
And set it down in the water for a planned
Rescue, but the smoking plane could not withstand

A sea landing. It would be a fiery crash landing.
So he ordered a parachute jump for his two crewmen.
"Hit the silk, hit the silk," he shouted again and again.
He waited as long as he could, hoping the men were safe, then
Bailed out and kept clear of the tail fin.
Lost to the depths were White, Delaney and the Avenger.
Two men sacrificed their lives to bring down the tower.

He dove out the plane, and cut his head on an elevator,
Opened his chute too early and plunged into the water.
Bush found his raft but faced immediate danger.
A Japanese boat sped toward him, intent on his capture.

If they captured him, he had no chance of surviving.
I would attack with low altitude strafing.
So I dived at the boat and set my guns blazing.
Quickly, fire engulfed the boat.

Bush was alone on his raft, miles from the carrier,
The day they destroyed the Chichi Jima tower.

Fifty miles away was the submarine Finback.
Its mission was to help aviators downed by flak
Who lost their planes in the morning attack.
Lt. Bush would be one of those they brought back.
As the hours passed, he grew increasingly weary
While paddling and drifting in the rolling sea.
He prayed that he would escape a briny
Fate and for a dramatic rescue by the US Navy.

He did not know the Finback was scanning the water,
Looking for a pilot who had bombed the tower.

The Finback found him alive but bloodied,
Pulled alongside, secured his raft and hoisted
Him on board. They saluted and welcomed
Bush who realized that his life had been saved.
He was taken to the Finback's bridge
And gave his account of the tower's damage.
The Captain sent the San Jacinto a message
And complimented the Lieutenant on his courage.

Someone took a picture of the young aviator
The day he bombed the Chichi Jima Tower.

* * * *

Off the Coast of Maine

For the earth shall be full of knowledge
Of the glory of the Lord
As the waters fill the sea. (Habakkuk 2:14)

Last evening's storm has dissipated.
Now the sea lies flat, calm this morning.
The horizon is partly obscured
By a light grey fog bank and low hanging
Clouds. Soft sunlight spreads from the rising sun
Spreading outward, casting a warming glow
Onto a cold and dark sleeping ocean.

Early-morning colors of red and yellow,
Mix with tinges of orange and violet
And meld with purples on the surface.
As we push the boat east at full throttle,
We rise and slam against a long roller
With a nerve jangling bang against the hull,
Then slide down the backside of a breaker.

Vikings and Basques sailed these same waters
Long ago in search of Conquest and Cod.
They were our earliest navigators
Before the Spaniards sailed in the name of God.
Today we may see Humpback or Finback whale,
And farther out fish for Haddock or Tuna,
Hear the ghostly warnings from Ishmael,
Or heed the story of ancient Jonah.

Here I am more alive than anyplace.
Physical cuts and bruises cure quickly.
The salty air is part of God's embrace.
Campaign stress dissipates. I am carefree.

A swell rises up from the ocean floor,
Crests then peaks, leans and falls forward and breaks,
Then attempts to regroup heading to shore.
The morning sun is up. It retakes
Its rightful place in the sky, driving night
Away from the seascape of fog and mist.

Everywhere we are warmed by sunlight.
Predawn chill and darkness are dismissed.
Off the Maine coast on the rolling ocean,
I sit with my sons enjoying the morning,
Just being here, enjoying God's creation.

* * * *

Betrayal

For too long, I have been the good soldier.
All this time, I have carried his water,
Defending, supporting and assuring
Our party faithful that he knew nothing
Of the White House Plumbers or Watergate.
He said the Press was trying to negate
His overwhelming landslide election
And destroy his hard won reputation.
He looked me straight in the eyes and said
He knew nothing of it until he read
The first story in the *Washington Post*
And became convinced his innermost
Associates were innocent as well.
He asked for me to help him dispel
The rumors and keep the party intact
While he put his agenda back on track.
At the time he was so believable,
I was unprepared for his deceitful
Lies. I was naive and too gullible,
Swallowing whole his plausible denial.

After that meeting, I fought the good fight,
Defending him to the nation despite
Growing concerns as to how much he knew.

Now tapes from his office are the breakthrough
Congress needs to bring an indictment
Against him and oust our government.
I drafted a letter today asking
Him to resign, and I will be sending
It to his office later today.
As I see it, he can no longer stay
In office. I am uncertain as to
How I should proceed. Will you please review
My letter and make corrections
As necessary. Do you have suggestions
On what I should do or what I should say?
He must resign. There is no other way.

So you think it best I hand the letter
To him. He is deflated. His posture
Suggests he is shrinking physically
And is withdrawing emotionally.
I could tell his mind was wandering
Yesterday at the Cabinet meeting.
Attacks by his enemies in the Press
Add fuel to impeachment talk in Congress.
Our party now faces a dark future.
We cannot let this drama continue.

Yesterday, I heard a troubling rumor
That one of the Watergate burglars
Has ties to New Orleans and Miami
As well as Dallas. This could prove risky
If congressional investigators
Take a year or longer to get answers
To an embarrassing list of questions
And try to establish connections
To past events, closed long ago,
Now resting in historical shadows.

Time is growing short. I will meet with him
As soon as possible. These times are grim.
I appreciate your advice. Thank you
For coming. There is nothing else to do.
As you depart, use the service door.
I forgot you had not been here before.

Yes, that is an original oil painting,
From Howard Hughes commemorating
Zapata Oil's first drilling success
In the Gulf of Mexico, a time of less
Complexity. Our end game now begins;
Nixon's presidency is at an end.

* * * *

First Base

The day is late
And shadows cross the infield.
We will meet our fate
On the diamond soon.
Baseball smells hang in the air:
Pine tar for the bats,
Sweat in the flannel uniforms

And old high top socks,
Shoes freshly blackened,
Rosin bags for the pitcher
And lyme marked foul lines.
Our gloves are oiled,
Caps curled just so.
Grass freshly mowed
Is baseball's incense.

It is top of the ninth
And we are hanging on.
Our lead is six to three.
They have two outs,
But they have men on
Second and third.

Our manager orders an intentional walk.
Now the tying run is on first.
Any base. Any base we call
For the final force out.
Their best hitter comes to the plate.
Everyone is nervous.

I spit on the dirt.
I spit on my glove.
I give a whistle,
Echoed by the third baseman.
A left-handed first baseman
Who can whistle is important
To the team. It reassures the pitcher.
Playing first base is one
Of a few places a left-hander
Has any advantage in the field.
I am ready.

Any base, any base. We call.
The lengthening shadows absorb
The building pressure.
I check and recheck the dirt in front of me,
Holding the runner close to the bag.

The batter is left handed
But we play him straight away
In the outfield.
The third baseman and I guard
The foul lines to protect against
An extra base hit.
The pitcher takes his wind up,
Swinging strike one. On the next pitch
I anticipate a hard ground ball
To me, but the Umpire
Calls Ball One which draws
Disapproval from the stands.
Ball Two brings a chorus of complaint.
The umpire is new to us and young.
His neck is red when he calls *Ball Three*
Amid a shower of boos from the stands.

The batter steps out of the box,
Looks at the third base coach
For a sign, and smiles as he
Steps back in the box.
No surprise here. He has the green light.
My mouth is dry. I cannot whistle.
Any base, any base, I croak.

The pitch is down the middle and the batter
Hits it hard over my head into
The right field corner.
Our right fielder has a long run to the ball.
The runners from second and third have scored.
The runner from first is headed into third
And gets a frantic wave to go home.
I run out to make the relay
To home plate.
I get the ball, pivot hard, and let
The ball fly toward home plate.
On one bounce, the ball reaches the catcher.
The runner slides to the plate.
Out. The runner is out. Everyone
Rejoices, jumps up and down.
We win 6–5. Everyone is pounding
One another. Oh, the joy of amateur
Victory. Pure and clean, wholesome joy.
Like no other.

* * * *

Seeking Lyndon's Advice on the Senate Race

With hat in hand, I asked to meet Lyndon
To seek his support in state politics.
At a his ranch, fifty miles from Austin,
He gave me a talk on Texas tactics.

I represent Houston in Congress,
But I want to be in the Senate,
So I asked him point blank to focus
On my chances to carry the state.

He said he will help me defeat Yarborough
If Lloyd Benson does not win the primary
Which is scheduled day after tomorrow.
He says he can support me secretly.

He said a Congressman eats chicken shit,
But chicken salad is a Senator's lunch.
He said the Senate is the home of leaders

Who often receive campaign gifts at brunch.

He will support me as a brave Westerner,
Or he might call me a Carpetbagger.

* * * *

My Favorite Par Three

Of all the great golf courses in the world,
Most are known for their signature par three's.

Among the many famous short golf holes,
Postage Stamp at Royal Troon can be deadly.

An errant shot there can destroy a round
And grant the hapless golfer a triple bogey.
After golf we retired to a Burns Supper
Which included haggis, neep, and tatties.
Haggis is made from sheep's heart and liver.
To eat it, you need a dram of whiskey.

Number twelve at Augusta is widely known
Because the Masters has such visibility.
The slightest puff of air over Rae's creek
Can dunk a bull into a slough of misery.
The air sparkles. Azalea and dogwood
Echo a long past Springtime when Arnie
Put together an unexpected charge
And recruited millions to his army.

The Duel hole at San Francisco Golf
Was the scene of a bitter tragedy
Where two men fought a duel to the death.
You sense their fear when you stand on the tee.
When the fog is in, and the air is still,
You can hear sounds from the shrubbery:
Voices counting paces, pistols being cocked,
Shots ringing out and cries of agony.

Number four, the par three, at National
Present fortifications of a military

Purpose. It is called a Redan hole
Because it repels assaults by the enemy.
Redan holes at Brookline and Shinnecock
Are fascinating challenges for me.
Add in Pinehurst, Riviera, and Sand Hills,
And you have the best Redans in the country.

For sheer drama and a stern test of golf
Sixteen at Cypress is where you want to be.
It looks like a mile across an inlet
To a green rising from a thundering sea.
The course was set in a primeval world
By the Scotsman Alistair Mackenzie
Who gave us some of our finest courses,
By allowing Nature to reveal Her Majesty.

When the wind blows and it rains at Pebble
The short downhill number seven can be
The cause of nightmares. It is on a downhill
Point where shots have fiendish variability.
Against the wind, a four iron can be short.
Club selection is a mystery.
When it is calm, a wedge can fly the green.
Your only hope is a knowledgeable caddy.

What is it that makes a golf course great?
Is it layout or physical beauty?
You need quality membership and staff
Led by a despotic Club Secretary.

So let me answer your question this way:
There are great short holes I have yet to see,
But my idea of perfection
Is standing on number ten at the Valley.
This course has always been a special place.
Built on sand hills in northern New Jersey,
Its ratings are atop the golfing world
For its course, management and privacy.

Each time I return, it is a grand experience.
I played there with some friends recently.
The night before our final round,

We went over to Mel's to play his par three.
On the way back, we stopped at the home
Of a man who showed us a club which he
Designed to hit a ball over a couch
And stop on the table adjacent his martini.

We started our last round on number ten,
Having been sent there by the starter, Lenny.
It took us awhile to get organized.
Soon we were joined by Billy and Rocky,
Who would be our wind and yardage consultants
After they finished their donuts and coffee.

They drove us out to Ten in a van.
We were silent as we drove through the trees.
The sun was up, but the grass was wet,
As we climbed up the hill to the tee.
Even though the hole is deceptively short,
It only plays as a downhill 130,
An impossible bunker guards the right front,
Named for a part of the Devil's anatomy.

We tossed golf tees to determine honors.
I had been partnered with Brady.
I thought I would hit my nine iron,
But I was handed a seven by Rocky.
That is too much club, I complained.
You were up late, and it is still early
Was the curt response I received.
Just keep your head down and swing smoothly.
The ball landed in the center of the green,
Stopped close to the pin, and I made a birdie.
Rocky began to mutter and stomped away.
Talking to himself, he said nothing to me.

That was the start of one of my best rounds,
So it is not too difficult to see
Why that short hole is my personal favorite
On that grand course in northern New Jersey.

* * * *

Rhetorical Questions

Once I sat in class in Grecian Gardens
Where I was tutored by Rhetoricians,
Learning standards of verbal eloquence,
While drilling on proficiency and practice.

I learned with great satisfaction
Standards for verbal repetition.
Through the efforts of Epistrophe
And the constant help of Epimone.
Then repetitions taught by Epizeuxis,
Revealed techniques from Epanalepsis.

Anaphora prefers only beginnings,
While Anadiplosis adds on endings.
Polysyndeton and Asyndneton
Argue over more or no conjunctions.
Poor Erotema had no answer
When asked which technique is better.
Appearing verbally schizophrenic,
Praetortio used linguistic
Sleight of hand, explaining a position
By not explaining, a mild deception.

Anadiplosis, help me speak.
My mind is exhausted, my body weak.
I lost her vote when I failed to kiss the baby.
I lost the husband's vote because of the lady.
I lost their friend's vote because they thought ill of me.
I lost the town's vote, the city's and the county's.
I lost the state's vote and finally the country's,
All for failing to kiss one baby, I lost the vote.

Come, relieve me mighty Epizeuxis
Take away this unfathomable distress.
Beaten, beaten, beaten,
I gave away this election.
Defeated, defeated, defeated,
Now, neither needed nor wanted.

Help me through this, Conduplico

Return me from the covering shadows.
Defeated, the word tightens my lungs, defeated.
Defeated, the word stirs bile within me, defeated.
Defeated, the word tightens the base of my skull, defeated.

Epimone, help me mitigate this disgrace,
By looking at it squarely in the face.
Saying aloud, I lost in California,
Saying aloud, I lost in Arizona,
Saying aloud, I lost in Nebraska.

I call on you Epanalepsis
Rescue me from total darkness.
The working press pushed hard against me,
Portrayed me as a privileged preppy,
Served as the mouthpiece of the other party.
My victory was stolen by the working press.

Be my guide Polyptoton,
Give me guidance and wisdom.
As a young man, I began my first campaign.
Since then, it has been endless campaigning.
Now I know that it is not a privilege to run for office.
It is the privileged who run for office.

Symploce use again your invisible wings
To help me through my emotional swings:
The first time, I was afraid to run for office.
The last time, I was afraid not to run for office.

There is beauty in rhetorical symmetry,
Reflected by the grace of Epistrophe:
The best course for our country
Is set by the Republican Party.
At its center are honesty and integrity,
Woven fabric of the Republican Party.
Winning in November requires party unity.
Sir, you will cause us to lose the Presidency.
You are destroying the Republican Party

Please join me on the podium Polysyndeton,
Join hands with Isocolon and Asyndeton.
Allow me to say most anything

JOHN KERR

As long as it is hard hitting
And endorses conservative positions,
And forces my opponents to answer questions,
And frustrates my opponents,
And carries political potence.

I have well-known positions.
I am opposed to abortion.
I endorse capital punishment.
I call for limited government.
I will appoint conservative judges.
I will not support new taxes.
I will keep prayer in our schools.
I will eliminate onerous business rules.

I will find wedge issues to
Bruise my opponent's reputation,
Confuse his supporters,
Use his words against him,
Subdue his contributors,
Argue with him through surrogates,
Woo his supporters,
Do damage to his campaign.

Reverse yourself, my friend Chiasmus
Put an end to this economic circus.

Everything was in balance, when I said no new taxes
The expense cart was hitched to the revenue horses.
Then expenses went out of control and unhitched the cart.
Previous agreements failed and came apart
Now the cart is ahead of the horses
They have the aces; I hold deuces
The American public is losing its patience.
Forced to raise taxes, I lost my balance.
It is time to end this economic circus.
I know you can do it, friend Chiasmus.

Shrewd Anastrophe and Cousin Hyperbaton
Your skillful knowledge I call upon.
Brave is the woman in the arena.

POEMS AND SONGS OF THE PRESIDENTS OF THE 20TH CENTURY

Brave is man living the drama.
Brave is the servant who leaves the moonless night,
Brave is the one who enters the glare of blinding light,
Brave is he who leaves the anonymous darkness,
Brave is she who joins the world of public service,
Brave are those who forsake a world of privacy,
Brave they are who live for the country.
Brave is the woman in the arena.
Brave is the man living the drama.

Reveal yourself to us, Aposiopesis
With your friends Praeteritio and Ellipsis.
Praeteritio, use the technique employed
In my speech to assure that I avoid
Direct accusations against my opponent
Which can be too direct and blatant.
I will not say anything derogatory,
That said his platform is a mystery.
I cannot say my opponent is a phony,
But his dissembling makes me angry.
And Aposiopesis, allow me to identify
A few deficiencies rather than supply
A complete list to the election pollsters
And independent, undecided voters.
My opponent lacks political courage.
His thinking is dealt straight from Cambridge.
I reject his stand on Capital Punishment
And the proper role of Government.
I can no longer endure this session,
And stand appalled by an itemization
Of his numerous errors of judgment.
I find his proposals so repugnant,
I am terminating this discussion.
To continue is out of the question.
Now is not the time to make us guess

Secretive intentions, dear Ellipsis.
Reveal to us the implied mystery,
And uncloak disguised identities.
Can truth endure in a campaign?
Only shades of it will reign.

JOHN KERR

Can a candidate become his own man?
As long as he listens to his adman.
Are attack advertisements beneficial?
Absolutely, to the advertising rabble.

I see you smile, Litotes, then smirk.
You think it is part of your work
To double up on negative thought,
Your victim bound up and caught
In a trap, a complicated, double
Maze of negative trouble.
At the debate, I did not find him uninformed.
Rather, I think his views have been formed
To present a pleasant, optimistic
Spin on a personality quite pessimistic.
I would not say he is uninteresting.
I would say he would be more interesting
To a gathering of morticians
Than a meeting of union electricians.

You can assist me Metanoia
To rid myself of this paranoia
That everyone uses my honesty
And curiosity against me.
I know, I know I should never
Speak out, or blurt out whatever
Is on my mind without taking
Time to do some critical thinking.
I was taught good manners, never to praise
Myself. I am sure it conveys
An inner strength, but it was used against
Me causing me a great deal of angst.
My personality is one of modesty and reflection,
Sound bites of loud voices gain attention.
In the future, I will be more direct
On some issues, while appearing circumspect
On others—No, I cannot be something
I am not, playing a role, or acting
Without intellectual honesty.

Erotema, how did I ever survive
My setback? Your questions helped revive

My campaign. How can any person
Say you never offer a solution?
How can one not see value in rhetorical
Questions versus a list of minimal
Suggestions? Are unanswerable questions
A foundation for all solutions?

Once I sat in class in Grecian Gardens
Where I was tutored by Rhetoricians,
Learning standards of verbal eloquence,
While drilling on proficiency and practice.

I learned with great satisfaction
Standards for verbal repetition.
Through the efforts of Epistrophe
And the constant help of Epimone.
Then repetitions taught by Epizeuxis,
Revealed techniques from Epanalepsis.

Anaphora prefers only beginnings,
While Anadiplosis adds on endings.
Polysyndeton and Asyndeton
Argue over more or no conjunctions.
Poor Erotema had no answer
When asked which technique is better.
Appearing verbally schizophrenic,
Praetortio used linguistic
Sleight of hand, explaining a position
By not explaining, a mild deception.

* * * *

Thoughts on a Winter Day by Mildred Kerr Bush (Millie)

Snoozing and dreaming of chasing squirrels,
Sunlight, winter warmth through the windows.
Big sleepy sigh, then a roll over,
One eye open; food in the bowl
Keeps me bonded with Her.

Shiny shoes and loud talk
Disturb my reverie.

JOHN KERR

I will lie on my back and see
If someone will stop and scratch me.

Most of my female friends are Springers
With proper, formal names
Which get informal shortened variations:
*Winifred becomes Winnie
Mildred becomes Millie.
Margaret becomes Maggie.
Susan becomes Suzie
Dorothy becomes Dolly.*

I have a son named Spot.
His name is a disgrace to me,
A lack of imagination,
It should have been Prescott.
He has my Roman nose;
He has my sweet breath and tongue;
He has my mouth and muzzle;
Best of all he has my feathers.

A silly dog named Benji
(née Benjamin) came to meet me
Today. Said he was a TV
Star. He stunk of perfume,
And rejected a slurp from the washroom.
Poor dumb dog is over groomed.

An intense odor from the scene
Of a previous accident,
Which was the cause of an
Overreaction by him, suggests
I should leave the carpet and go
Outdoors to relieve myself
And chase squirrels.

I stand at the door. He sees me,
He talks to the shoes, ignores me.
I scratch at the door and bark.
She comes to the door,
And speaks to me, encourages me
To get the squirrel, the hated brown one

Who taunts me,
Who mocks me from the tree.
Blood lust overcomes me.

I go crazy.
I am excited, barking
Twirling around, whining
Then she launches me out the door
Toward the torpid squirrel.

* * * *

Irony

Talks on intercontinental missiles
Between me and an aging actor
Led to talks on growing vegetables
Between you and an ex-Combine driver.
How ironic that my scarlet birthmark,
Which some religious believed a sign,
Would become my political trademark,
A heavenly forecast from the divine.
Pulling back from the edge of destruction,
I leapt like a Spirit from the Bolshoi,
Tossing a confetti of corruption
Spread by a mad character from Tolstoy.
That action was one of a Romanoff,
Not Mikhail Sergeyevich Gorbachev.

* * * *

WILLIAM JEFFERSON CLINTON
President 1993-2001

Introduction:
Thinking about William Jefferson Clinton

He worked hard over long hours,
He insisted that those around him
Do the same. Meetings with him
Seemed to never end. Hour
After hour would pass before
Any resolution would appear.

Brilliance
He was the smartest man in the room.
We were the students in his classroom.

Appetites
It was inner hunger that seemed to drive.
His decisions and set his will to survive.

Feelings
No one could resist his personal appeal.
Feel your pain? The emotion was real.

Terminations
He was bad at personnel terminations,
But he was great at Presidential pardons.

Charm
When he talked, you and he connected.
Even the toughest of his critics melted.

* * * *

Wedding Day

She needed some time before she said yes
To my proposal that we should marry.
She felt there were issues we should address
Prior to our wedding. Finally, she
Felt sufficiently comfortable
With our agreements and me as her husband.
We were married at my house in Fayetteville
With my brother Roger serving as best man.
At a friend's home, we held a reception
For our friends and the law school faculty.
We toasted them on the two acre lawn
And served cake from a local bakery.

In step with current feminine fashion,
She plans to keep her maiden name Rodham.

* * * *

Partners.
Hillary and Bill Clinton decide to govern as Copresidents prior to taking office.
She will focus on domestic problems, and he will handle international situations.

My Strategy

I hear George Bush's popularity
Is so great that my opponents are ending
Bids to head the Democratic Party
Just before the primaries are starting.
That is great news for my nomination.
It will keep large donors on the sidelines,
And then allow a new generation
To get newspaper stories and headlines.

POEMS AND SONGS OF THE PRESIDENTS OF THE 20TH CENTURY

We will get television coverage
On the deteriorating economy,
And I will bring a message of courage
And hope to an anxious, troubled country.
My message will be one of unity.
I will campaign for economic justice
And work to implant racial harmony.
I will bring hope to those called hopeless.
I will drive a sharp political wedge
Between the rich and those less privileged.

* * * *

The first family in the White House.

269

JOHN KERR

We Will Govern as Equal Partners

We will govern as Equal Partners.
She will coordinate the White House lawyers,
And I will deal with foreign leaders.
She will supervise health care planners
While I get control of union leaders
So we can govern as Equal Partners.

She is as smart as any white shoe lawyer;
She can hold her ground with business brokers
And firmly dismiss publicity seekers.
She will appoint foreign ambassadors
And half of the cabinet members
With the help of her feminist sisters
In our first term as Equal Partners.

I enjoy dealing with Wall Street bankers.
I speak the language of financiers
And deal easily with complex numbers.
I can hold my own with large investors
And explain budgetary numbers.
I can discern political figures
Constructed by unscrupulous pollsters.
We are qualified as Equal Partners.

How will I be judged in the future?
I hope better than my predecessors.
Out of office their legacies suffer.
Kennedy spent time with Vegas mobsters
Who helped him be a womanizer.
Lyndon Johnson was enthralled with Hoover
Who fed him dirt on Kennedy's backers.
Nixon was an unethical liar
Who was as paranoid as Edgar Hoover.
Carter talks like a Sunday Schoolteacher
Or a Bible-thumping gospel preacher.

Reagan is captured by Astrologers
And sits in a daze with old movie stars.
Poor sweet Bush acts like an East Coast boater
Or an upper crust country club golfer.

I think when we retire in the future,
We will be known as effective partners.

We will learn the benefits and pleasures
Of the office. Movers and shakers
From all industries will be here: Actors,
Dancers, Entertainers and Performers.
We will host America's winners.
We will enjoy private jets and chauffeurs,
And I will enjoy evening pleasures:
Pizza, private screenings, beer, and cigars.
Our needs will be met by cooks and butlers,
Catered to by stylists and tailors.

We will enjoy the fruits of our labors.
Our stories will be sought by publishers
Who want to know us as Equal Partners
As we lay the groundwork for our futures.
I would not be here if it were not for her.
Our future could not be brighter.

* * * *

Complete the Nominations

You are past the deadline for nominees
In key roles to be named. Employees
Of your new administration languish
For lack of decisions. Sir, finish
These late-night bull sessions.
Make your choices and announce your selections.
You are like the broke gambler in Hot Springs
Studying his tout sheets at the railings
Hoping one more glance at the racing form
With his paddock friends can somehow transform
His life with one big bet on the right horse.
Now there are more horses on your racecourse
Than openings at the Starter's Gate.
Get on with the program; end this debate.
This dithering is wasting your political capital
On committee opinion and babble.
It is now time to end the discussions.

Wrap them up. Announce your decisions.

* * * *

Get the Press off My Back

I may have had the shortest Honeymoon
On record for a first-term President.
From the start, the Press began to impugn
Motives for my trips, everywhere I went.
They got on me for letting Hillary
Use *Air Force One* to get a haircut
In New York. After that, they got on me
When I got my haircut on a visit
To Los Angeles, keeping *Air Force One*
Parked for an hour on the tarmac
While I got styled in the aft cabin.
The Press made it sound as if air traffic
Was disrupted. No one handles the Press
Well for me, especially Stephanopolis.

* * * *

Tactics to Conclude Dayton Negotiations

No progress has been made here in Dayton.
It seems they want to delay and prolong
The talks in hopes the negotiations
Bog down, and we become headstrong
To the point that we look the other way,
Ignoring so-called ethnic cleansing
And pack up our bags in the next few days.
If we leave, they will resume mass killing
And executions in Sarajevo.
They plan to murder defenseless Muslims
And deliver a merciless deathblow
To thousands of innocent victims.
I plan to force their hand when we convene
By showing a film of an F-16.

* * * *

Reaction to the State of the Union Speech Delivered on January 24, 1995

Come in, come in. I am glad you are here.
Reaction to last night's speech appears
To be unanimously favorable.
The minute I walked down the aisle,
I knew something special was happening.
The Congress was electric and buzzing
With hopeful anticipation
As I stood to address the nation.

I think you are the only person who
Knew what I was trying to do.
You and I must follow up to seize
This day, making sure our message carries
To people who live outside Washington
On farms and in cities of the nation.

My staff tells me it was the longest State
Of the Union speech on record, too late
For most of the television viewers
And the East Coast commentators.
The speech ran an hour and three quarters.
Its length was an embarrassment to my advisors,
But I had a lot to say, and I wanted
Major parts of the speech to be quoted
And reviewed in the national press.
Now everyone considers it a success,
Except for some Dole and Gingrich grumbling
And the usual partisan whining.

You should have seen some of the crowd's faces
As the time passed. Suppressed urges
For a toilet break kept them twisting
And turning in their chairs, then applauding
Wildly in hopes that I might be nearing
What they thought might be the end of the speech.
In those last minutes, I tried to preach
Directly to the hearts and minds of our
People. It felt right even though the hour
Was late. I had been interrupted

By applause so many times it delayed
The evening, but I took their energy,
And with their help, I spoke to the country.
These are the thoughts I wanted them to hear.
My message to America is clear:

Our plans will focus on the middle class.
We will provide it with tools to surpass
Achievements of previous generations
While they restart our economic engines.

We live in dangerous times. Security
At home and abroad are priorities
As we seek ways to stop terrorism
While living in a country of freedom.

We will support our allies and partners
And keep good relations with our neighbors.
I explained why we should help Mexico
With guarantees to shore up the Peso.

Our strength is the American family.
We must guarantee them health security
And provide them with opportunity,
By cutting red tape and bureaucracy.
My message was one of hope and progress.
I said our best days are ahead of us.
That theme will continue to resonate,
And it will become our midterm mandate.
Please leave by the side door as usual.
You make my staff jealous and resentful.

* * * *

Here Come the '94 Midterms

With all due respect, you have lost voters
Because first term political blunders
Obscure exceptional accomplishments,
Such as Haiti and the Jordon Peace Agreements.
Your failed efforts on Health Care Reform
Have created a political firestorm

Because your advisors failed to gauge
The electorate's mood and gave front page
Headlines to your most vocal opponents.
I urge you, remain in Washington.
Campaign if you must, from behind the curtain
Of the Office. If you go glad handing
In each important state, politicking
And joy riding, it will spell disaster.
Chances for a second term will be over.

Charlie

* * * *

You Are Dead Wrong, Charlie

I saved your note to rub it in your face.
Read my response. Put it in a safe place.
You cannot be correct. You are dead wrong.
We are going to rebound. All along
You have been negative. I know these things.
My staff tells me we are on an upswing.
Your polls are as wrong as they can be.
Your forest is hidden by polling trees.
Tomorrow morning we will at last know,
And you, sir, will be eating day-old crow.

* * * *

We Lost the Midterms

We have lost the election countrywide.
House and Senate—gone in a landslide
It appears that we lost eight Senators
And fifty-four or five Representatives.
George Bush is the next Texas governor.
In New York, Cuomo will be a goner.
It looks like New Gingrich is the winner.

Charlie

* * * *

JOHN KERR

Spring House Cleaning after the Midterms

I made some mistakes in my first two years,
But the biggest of all was listening
To my advisors. Now I must shift gears
And make a new start. This team loves blaming
Anyone, except themselves, for the loss.
So I will sit with Hillary and make a list
Of those whom I keep and those whom I toss.
The largest number will be those dismissed.
To think I did what they told me to do,
And then for them to turn around and claim
It was my fault shows they have no clue
Why we lost. I will not accept the blame.

The problem was that I did not have a good plan
To communicate all our achievements.
If the people failed to understand
Our most significant accomplishments
On whose shoulders should the fault be placed?
A good communication strategy
Is crafted to assure the country gets it.
Out goes the bath water and the baby.
They face a simple choice: be fired or quit.

Now I must act Presidential and wait
For the Republicans to run aground.
And the conservative tide to abate.
The Comeback Kid will be re crowned.

* * * *

Al Gore and Newt Gingrich applaud as President Clinton waves during the State of the Union address in 1997.

A Day of Horror

*Steel the mind.
Turn off thoughts.
Suppress emotions.
Focus on the task.
Quiet thinking.
Live free or die.*

*The moment is at hand.
The slaughter at Ruby Ridge
Will not be forgotten.
Today is the anniversary
Of the burning of children
At Mt. Carmel near Waco.
In their name,
I am the Avenger.
Planning is complete.
Action is now.*

JOHN KERR

Live free or die.

Walk away from the truck.
No expression.
Stay calm.
Vengeance is mine.
Live free or die.

Sir, pardon this interruption,
But there has been an explosion
Today in Oklahoma City
Where many federal agencies
Are housed. Investigators
Are there looking for answers,
We know it was an act of terrorism
That will claim countless victims.

I have escaped.
No time for celebration.
Drive north.
Take a breath.
Watch for trouble.
I am Free.

We have a chopper overhead.
We can see wounded and dead
Being pulled from the rubble.
The scene below is terrible.
Rescue teams have arrived
Searching for those who survived.

Doctor, we are minutes from St. Anthony.
Others are headed to Baptist or university.
Place your Triage unit in the driveway.
Some victims need immediate surgery.

A patrol car is tailing me.
He wants me to pull over.
Stay calm,
Stay calm.
He will let me go.
No way for him to know.

Sir, your vehicle does not have a plate
Which is against the law in this state.
And your permit to carry a weapon
Applies to Kansas. I must bring you in
Under arrest and ask one of the judges
To decide on the specific charges.

Stay calm.
No way to connect me
To the explosion.

Sir, we know the killer's identity,
And by chance we have him in custody.
The FBI traced the rental truck
To him, and with a stroke of luck,
We found him in an Oklahoma jail,
Where he was trying to make bail
On charges of a traffic violation
And carrying a concealed weapon.

* * * *

Death of a Rock and Roll Prophet

Early this morning, I got the message
You needed my assessment of the damage
Done at the Branch Davidian compound.
I had been here two days in the background,
Waiting for the assault operation
To begin. There were women and children
In there, but the talks showed no progress,
And more delay could jeopardize our success.

I used my White House pass to get close.
First, they brought up equipment to bulldoze
Parts of the house and then fired canisters
Of tear gas into the buildings hoping
For surrender, but both sides kept shooting.

A steady breeze began in late morning,

And for a brief moment it shifted
And blew back the gas until it covered
Me where I stood. The pain was so intense
I could not breathe. Gas filled my senses,
And I collapsed, gasping for air, vomiting
My lunch. My nose and throat began burning
As if they were on fire. I struggled
To stand erect, and the wind shifted
Away from me, back toward the compound.
Where the assault tanks continued to pound
At the buildings. A little after noon
I saw smoke rising from the commune.

Within minutes, the compound was engulfed
In flames. I saw a man who attempted
To escape, but one of the sharp shooters
Shot him as he ran toward the snipers.
The wind whipped the fire into a frenzy.
Those trapped in there met a fiery
Death. From what I saw there are no survivors.

This operation is a series of blunders,
And can be a public relations nightmare,
So find a scapegoat for the press and declare
Koresh, the leader, a child molester.
Play up the multiple wives, drugs and guns,
His crackpot doctrines and his cache of weapons.

At the Hilton bar, I watch the nightly news
To see if anyone can find an excuse
For what we did to these hapless pilgrims
Who followed this guy and became victims,
Caught between their prophet and the authorities,
An Old Testament standoff between the armies
Of Satan and their tribal Messiah
Who was their rock-and-roll Jeremiah.

****

Ode for a Fallen Warrior

In state, here lies a son of Solomon
Sent directly from the line of David.
In peace, he served as his nation's statesman.

In war, he was never defeated.
A victim of a fanatical zealot,
His body lies here, mortally wounded.

He was Israel's modern-day prophet,
A visionary, a secular king.
He could chide us, then lift our spirits.

For several years, he has been leading
The Middle East toward resolution
Of dividing issues that are keeping
Nations hostile to each other. Aaron
Knew he had to march out and cross over
Jordon or else there would be no Zion.

So Yitzhak stepped into our future.
In the wind, he heard God's command
To lead His people, like his ancestor,
Into the long-awaited promised land.
Our God spared Yitzhak's/Isaac's life,
Halting the dagger in Abraham's hand.

This time God did not stay the assassin's knife.
Yitzhak is his martyred sacrifice.

* * * *

Five Frozen Margaritas, No Salt

You have made a sensible case that we
Must move to rescue our NAFTA partner
Or be seen in the eyes of history
As heartless, unreliable bankers.
Your analysis of the situation
Is compelling. They need loan guarantees
To avoid economic devastation

And a financial hemispheric crisis.
With this commitment of thirty billion,
If I find you bailing out someone there,
Such as your old employers at Goldman,
You will spend the rest of your days on welfare.

I told Daschle, Dole, Newt, and Gephardt
Your margarita rim contains no salt.

* * * *

A Lesson from Judges

I think of sin as making bad choices
Between evil and what the book teaches.
A close reading of the Book of Judges
Shows a path to escape Satan's clutches.

Bad choices put me in sea of trouble.
I have more problems than I am able
To find answers. What I did is shameful.
I sit alone in the keep of this castle.

Logical consequences cause despair
So painful I cannot repair
My life. Oh God, please help remove this snare.
Show me a way and answer my prayer.

If you will send me counsel who is wise,
I will follow his teaching and devise
Honest plans I can follow to rise
From these depths. Please, God, end this crisis.

* * * *

Thank You for Your Service

Thank you so much for being a faithful
Friend and assistant to me for eight years.
As my time to leave the White House nears,
Please accept this folder for your loyal
Service to me. The folder contains poems

Written to and by me. Some are gems,
While others are just plain awful.
In the years to come, you will enjoy
Recalling meetings, when you as a houseboy
Would record aside comments at the table
When I excused myself to take a call.

These other folders contain personal
Reflections which could be hurtful
To the authors. Therefore I will keep them
Safe in this folder marked Secret Poems.

* * * *

In Case You Think I Am Leaving

In case you think I am leaving,
You should think it over.
I plan to be here again
With my political partner.

She will be our President
After W's term is over,
I will do whatever it takes.
I will be her campaign manager.

It may take a term or two
Or it may take longer,
I will become a statesman,
So I can help elect her.

I will build a library
Where I can give lectures
On important political topics
That affect our nation's future.

People will return to us.
We will speak for all the Boomers.
No one can defeat us.
This will be our great Adventure.

* * * *

A READER'S GUIDE TO THE POEMS

Introduction

During the early part of the twentieth century, the United States of America began transitioning from a rural, agriculturally based society to an urban, manufacturing based society. Against a background of periodic economic expansions followed by economic retractions, the nation was never free very long from war or rumors of war. In this century the United States became a major world power.

The first president of the twentieth century was William McKinley, a former Civil War officer, from Ohio. The last president of the century was William Jefferson Clinton of Arkansas. Between them sixteen presidents guided the nation.

Three generations of the same family worked continuously in the Executive Mansion, later the White House, throughout the century. They collected poems written to, from, and about the presidents. The poems they collected highlight personal struggles, triumphs, and defeats of the presidents.

The first of these men who collected poems was named Robert whose deceased father had served with President McKinley at Antietam during the Civil War. After his father died, Robert secured a menial job at the Executive Mansion and moved from Ohio to Washington. He began work in the stables and later found work in the main house.

George Cortelyou, McKinley's personal secretary, helped Robert learn his duties. Cortelyou took an interest in Robert, and he gave the young man an old leather box that had belonged to President Ulysses Grant. He told Robert to collect odds and ends that no one wanted, such as ticket stubs, campaign buttons or letters that were to be thrown away. He pointed out that people would send the president poems from time to time, and he should keep those he found interesting. He also mentioned that the president had written several poems. Robert followed Cortelyou's advice and began his collection of presidential memorabilia.

Following McKinley's assassination in 1901, Robert remained an employee in the Executive Mansion. He served a total of six presidents: William McKinley, Theodore Roosevelt, William Howard Taft, Woodrow Wilson, Warren Harding and Calvin Coolidge. Robert retired after Coolidge left office in 1928.

His son James took possession of the old leather box and succeeded Robert. James continued the tradition of keeping interesting odds and ends and poems.

In time, James served six presidents before he retired. They were Herbert Hoover, Franklin Roosevelt, Harry Truman, Dwight Eisenhower, John Kennedy and Lyndon Johnson. When James retired, he was succeeded by his son John. John continued to work in the White House, as had his father and grandfather. While there, John served Richard Nixon, Gerald Ford, Jimmy Carter, Ronald Reagan, George Bush and William Clinton.

John maintained the family tradition of collecting presidential odds and ends, but he tended to keep poems and press clippings more often. Near the end of his time in the White House, he gave away most of the miscellaneous contents of the box, but he kept the collected poetry of eighteen presidents.

An Old Man Receives a Visitor

An Old Man, in his bed in a nursing home, welcomes a visitor who has come to see him. The Old Man was born in 1905 and is nearing his final days. He lived in Washington DC, and he knew Robert, James, and John well. His visitor asks for him to recount stories of the presidents that he knew and share stories of the three men who worked in the White House.

A Reception in the White House (January 1929)

At his retirement reception, James summarizes how he got to Washington and his years in the White House.

****

William McKinley

As a young man McKinley was drawn into the Civil War from his native Ohio. He was a good leader during the war. At the Battle of Antietam, he showed courage in battle. After the Civil War, he returned to Ohio and became a lawyer. He served in the Congress. He was elected governor of Ohio, and he became the twenty-fifth president. While president, he guided the country during the war with Spain. The victory over Spain brought the United States into prominence as a world power. Campaigning for a second term, he asked Theodore Roosevelt to be his vice president. He campaigned from his front porch in Ohio against the populist William Jennings Bryan.

During McKinley's presidency, large trusts dominated oil, transportation and the economy. McKinley was supported by the trusts in his bid for reelection. The men who ran the trusts distrusted Roosevelt who was causing them trouble in New York where he was governor. The men behind the trusts pushed McKinley to get Roosevelt out of the way by naming him the vice presidential nominee, a dead-end job at the time. McKinley was assassinated in Buffalo, New York, in 1901. Theodore Roosevelt became the youngest president in the history of the United States.

The Modern Campaign of 1900

Mark Hannah, a powerful Republican, is the speaker in this dramatic monologue. It is set in the Executive Mansion as McKinley begins to raise money for his reelection campaign. Attending the meeting are John D. Rockefeller, Andrew Carnegie, John Pierpont Morgan and Cornelius Vanderbilt. McKinley does not attend the meeting, but he watches the proceedings from a window.

In this dramatic monologue, Mark Hanna makes the case for McKinley's second term, and solicits money.

The Hurricane of 1900 at Galveston, Texas.
The Sestina of Isaac Cline and
A Tragic Hurricane on the Gulf Coast

The island town of Galveston, Texas, was hit by a devastating hurricane in 1900. Isaac Cline was the head of the weather bureau in Galveston when the hurricane hit the unsuspecting town on the Gulf of Mexico. The author of the sestina is Isaac Cline. The extent of the hurricane was not known until reports began coming in from Texas. Robert retrieved this poem from McKinley's personal files after Roosevelt took office.

A Tragedy in Buffalo and
Eulogy of William McKinley

The tragic death of William McKinley in Buffalo, New York, caused great suffering and pain to those who worked with him and to the nation. George Cortelyou, McKinley's personal secretary, delivered the eulogy, and he gave it to Robert for safekeeping.

Caring for Ida McKinley and
Ida's Sonnet

Ida McKinley suffered from depression and physical problems. The sonnet reflects her pain from the loss of her two children. McKinley was patient with her and curtailed many public functions to care for her.

They Executed McKinley's Assassin

This poem explores the thoughts of the assassin. McKinley's assassin, Leon Czolgosz, was under the influence of Emma Goldman, a radical from Chicago. Czolgosz states that all authority is the enemy.

Ballade of Leon Czolgosz

The assassin was tried, found guilty, and executed following McKinley's death. Czolgosz had hoped that other leaders would be assassinated. This poem follows the classic French form of the ballade.

My Father Gave Me This from the Civil War

Robert describes how he got the long narrative of Stone Mountain and Antietam and McKinley's role in the battles.

Stone Mountain and Antietam–1862

This long narrative poem is part of a much larger work written by an unnamed companion of McKinley during his Civil War days. It is the story of a march south from Washington and the battles of Stone Mountain and Antietam. The larger work had been lost by the time it came into Robert's possession.

McKinley showed bravery in combat at Antietam where twenty-two thousand men on both sides were casualties in one day of battle. Mechanized instruments of war against frontal assaults of infantry and cavalry were a prelude to tactics of World War I.

* * * *

Theodore Roosevelt

Theodore Roosevelt captured the attention of the American public with his vigor in the execution of his duties as President. He was energetic, and he was not afraid to speak his mind on matters he thought important. He was familiar with the classics and current authors. He was a sophisticated amateur historian, and he was a prolific author. He was a man of letters and a man of action.

As governor of New York, Roosevelt was handed the vice presidency at the insistence of the men who controlled large trusts of oil, railroads and shipping. After he became vice president he thought about attending law school. He thought he would have plenty of spare time, and he would need a job when his term was over.

Roosevelt learned politics in the New York legislature after he graduated from Harvard. Later he tried ranching in the Dakotas. Returning to New York, he worked as a civil service commissioner and then as New York City police commissioner. Later he was appointed undersecretary of the navy.

At the start of the Spanish-American war, he organized a cavalry unit comprised of eastern polo players and western ranchers. The unit became known as the Rough Riders and gained fame in Cuba at San Juan Hill. He was elected governor of New York on the strength of his fame as a Rough Rider.

The poems below were collected by Robert during his time working in the Roosevelt administration. They present a picture of his wide-ranging interests and explain his philosophy of life.

Two Strong Wills

Robert explains the tension between John Singer Sargent and Roosevelt as Sargent attempts to paint Roosevelt's portrait.

John Singer Sargent Paints
Theodore Roosevelt's Portrait–1903

John Singer Sargent was the most famous portrait painter of his day. Both he and Roosevelt were strong personalities. His attempt to get Roosevelt to sit for a painting was exasperating for Sargent. Roosevelt enjoyed the contest, and he made it difficult for Sargent to work.

This poem parallels Sargent's and Roosevelt's attitudes in two separate letter poems someone found and placed side by side. The poem concludes that Sargent's work is excellent. At the end of the process, both Sargent and Roosevelt think the painting is excellent.

The President Suggested a Reading Program and
a Letter to My Young Friend

The poem is from Roosevelt to a young person who asked for recommendations on what to read. The identity of the young friend is not stated, but it may have been Robert who was seeking ways to improve his position. Roosevelt had strong opinions on authors and works he liked and disliked. He called Mark Twain a prized idiot.

Jefferson Davis Wrote to President Roosevelt and
an Open Letter to Jefferson Davis

President Roosevelt asked Robert to edit his response to a letter from Jefferson Davis asking for Roosevelt to cease attacking him in the papers.

Roosevelt considered Robert E. Lee to be an honorable man who fought for his side in the Civil War. In contrast, he called Jefferson Davis, president of the Confederacy, a traitor and refused to meet with him or to refrain from attacking him in the press.

Money, an Inner Conflict and Thinking
about the Nobel Prize

Roosevelt enjoyed the prestige of winning the Nobel Prize for brokering a peace between Japan and Russia, but he was conflicted over whether he should accept the financial remuneration that accompanied the award.

In a letter poem to his son, Roosevelt explains that he will accept the honor but refuse the money that accompanies it. He felt he was doing his duty in helping bring the war between Russia and Japan to a conclusion. Roosevelt was not a wealthy man, and he could have used the money, but he felt he could not accept it. .

Theodore Roosevelt and His Rough Riders

The men whom Roosevelt led at San Juan Hill in Cuba became known as the Rough Riders. He offered to raise another group of Rough Riders during World War I. President Wilson said he would consider authorizing the Rough Riders if Roosevelt promised to be killed in battle.

Ode to the Rough Riders

Theodore Roosevelt had great respect for the horsemen from the West. He continued to honor them during his presidency. He helped them after the war.

Living at the Edge Roosevelt believed that exertion and mental toughness were required by individuals to keep the nation strong.

Live the Strenuous Life

This poem spells out Roosevelt's vigorous approach to life. It is based on a speech he gave to the Hamilton Club and later writings. His adolescence years were marked by frailty and poor eyesight. He overcame his weaknesses and willed himself to be a mentally and physically fit man. The words are Roosevelt's, but the poem's author is unknown.

Consequences of the Strenuous Life
(Vigor di Vita)

In later life, Roosevelt suffered from his daring adventures. Roosevelt was blinded in one eye from a boxing match in the White House.

Roosevelt died from an infection that he contracted on a trip in South America. He had hoped to run for another term, but the infection ruined those plans.

Former President Roosevelt Toured the West

Roosevelt took an extended trip to Africa and Europe after he left office. He returned to the United States, and then toured the western states to avoid the political intrigues of Washington.

The Ousel

From earliest childhood, Roosevelt loved birds. He wrote about them, and he studied them all of his life. On a trip to Yellowstone, he saw an Ousel and wrote a letter about it. Someone unknown wrote the poem which Robert put in the old leather box. Ousel is the way Roosevelt spelled the word. It is a variation of Ouzel, a European bird.

The Hopi Snake Dance

While traveling in the West, Roosevelt attended a Hopi snake dance ceremony. The poem is about respect for the powers of Nature. Roosevelt told this story to a companion who put it into poetic form.

Navaho Sunset

A sunset in Arizona can be a magnificent visual experience. Roosevelt traveled there, and here he reflects on the sunset in the land of the Navaho. The author of the poem is unknown.

William Howard Taft

William Howard Taft was pushed into running for president at the insistence of his mother, wife, brother and President Roosevelt. He was trained as a lawyer, then rose to the office of solicitor general. He served as governor of the Philippines following the Spanish American war.

He wanted to be chief justice of the Supreme Court, but Roosevelt and Taft's wife Nellie convinced him to run for president in 1908. Roosevelt supported him and campaigned for him.

After Taft was in the White House, Roosevelt began to have misgivings about Taft and regretted that he had backed him. Eventually, Roosevelt turned against Taft and challenged him at the Republican convention in Chicago in 1912. Taft won the nomination, but Roosevelt bolted the party and established the Progressive Party, which came to be known as the Bull Moose Party. The division enabled the victory of the Democratic Party nominee, Woodrow Wilson.

After Dinner in the White House Library–1906

This poem is based on a meeting of President Roosevelt, Mrs. Taft and William Howard Taft after dinner in the White House to determine the course for Taft. Would Taft become president or chief justice? Robert served coffee and listened at the door for an answer.

Governor of the Philippines and in the Philippines

After the war with Spain, Taft was appointed governor. The first poem sets the stage for the second poem.

The second poem is based on an exchange between secretary of War, Elihu Root, and Taft when he was governor of the Philippines. Later, Taft told the story on himself. Taft's consumption of large quantities of food became a problem for him. He gained weight, and his inability to stay awake after a heavy meal became legendary.

A Long Relationship with Yale and Yale Lies Deep in My Bones

These poems trace the many ties of William Howard Taft to Yale University. His father had been a student in 1829. Taft was an undergraduate there. Later he was offered the presidency of the school, and he was a law professor there after he left the White House.

The Pleasures of Golf

Taft used golf as an escape from the White House. He did not break 100 as a general rule, but he was an avid golfer with his aide, Archie Butt.

Cherry Blossoms

Nellie Taft had admired cherry trees in blossom in Japan when she was visiting there. She ordered trees for the Capitol basin while Taft was in the White House. The mayor of Tokyo presented them as a gift to the United States.

Taft Came Under Attack and Stop the Bull Moose

Roosevelt launched a verbal attack on Taft. Roosevelt bolted from the Republican convention in Chicago, forming the Bull Moose Party.

In Stop the Bull Moose, the ballade expresses the frustration of mainline Republicans with the disruption of the convention in 1912. The author is Elihu Root who was chairman of the convention. Loss of Roosevelt's friendship and support bothered Taft a great deal. Their long-standing friendship was broken. Wilson eventually won the election.

A Dream Realized during the Harding administration, Harding nominated Taft to be chief justice.

Court Is in Session–1922

William Howard Taft, as chief justice of the United States Supreme Court, looked around the court room. Finally, he had achieved the position he always wanted. It was everything he had dreamed.

* * * *

Woodrow Wilson

Woodrow Wilson was a staunch Presbyterian and an academic who became president of Princeton University. Following his academic career, he was governor of New Jersey, and he became the Democratic nominee for president in 1912.

The Republican Party was in disarray. Roosevelt had become disenchanted with William Howard Taft, his handpicked successor, and challenged him at the Republican convention in Chicago. Taft won the backing of the party, and Roosevelt bolted the convention. He established the Progressive Party, which later became known as the Bull Moose Party. Taft and Roosevelt polled seven million votes between them, but Wilson was an easy winner. The Democrats took a majority in the Senate and the House of Representatives.

Wilson was president at a difficult time in the history of the United States. War broke out in Europe during his first term, but he kept the United States out of the conflict until his second term. At the end of the war, Wilson supported the newly formed League of Nations which he believed would keep western nations out of war.

In helping to form the League of Nations, Wilson was opposed by the Republicans. Senator Henry Cabot Lodge was the primary leader against the League. The main objection to the League of Nations was that only the United States Congress had the power to declare war.

Wilson campaigned endlessly for the Treaty. He was in the West trying to drum up support for the Treaty when he had a debilitating stroke which hampered him until the end of his presidency.

War Speeches to Congress

President Wilson reestablished the custom of directly addressing Congress on important matters. These were two speeches he gave to Congress. The first asked for a declaration of war on April 2, 1917. The second notified the Congress of the end of hostilities in 1918.

An Influenza Pandemic and the Forgotten Plague of 1918–1919

One of the most horrible plagues in the history of the world happened in a two-year span near the close of the war in Europe. The influenza virus mutated into a virulent form and, two years later, mutated out. It confounded all known medical science at the time. Even President Wilson got a case of the flu. Because of the weariness of the war and its rapid disappearance, it was soon forgotten within a brief period of time.

Victory Celebrations and We Are Marching Home

The nation celebrated the end of the war in Europe. "We Are Marching Home" is a song written for returning troops from the war in Europe. They had departed as farm boys, but they returned home as men to face an uncertain future. A tenor, a baritone, and a bass sing it with a refrain for all.

My Introduction to Mathematics

Robert and Albert Einstein discuss the concepts of time while Einstein waits to meet President Wilson.

The Garden of Mathematical Delights and the Election of 1912: A Pastoral Poem

This long poem used the results of the 1912 presidential election to reaffirm the theorem of Pythagoras. A pastoral, it has the classic elements of a poem of this type, including shepherds, shepherdesses, an idyllic setting and noble themes.

In this poem, a prodigy is welcomed to the garden and given an assignment. There are obscure references, and plays on words, puns, mathematical references and puzzling phrases in the poem.

Final Lecture—1924 Edith Galt, Wilson's second wife, wrote this eulogy. It summarizes his good work and devotion to the principles of democracy.

* * * *

Warren G. Harding

A newspaperman from Marion, Ohio, Harding entered politics and rose to become a Republican senator. At the convention of 1912, Harding remained loyal to the party and supported Taft over Roosevelt.

During Woodrow Wilson's term as president, Harding objected to the League of Nations. At the Republican convention in hot and steamy Chicago in 1920, the three primary candidates were unable to win a majority of the delegates through seven ballots. With time running out, Harding was selected by party king makers and was named the Republican nominee.

Harding was a handsome man. He was not a polarizing personality, and he won the presidency with a *Back to Normalcy* slogan and theme. He died suddenly in office in 1923 while on a visit to Alaska and the west coast. He was popular in the country at the time.

After his death, a series of personal and political scandals captured the attention of the press and the public, causing much harm to Harding's reputation as a public figure.

Listening to Senator Harding

Harding addressed the Senate on his opposition to the League of Nations while President Wilson was touring the western states.

Senator Harding Addresses the Senate, September 11, 1919

This poem shows the extreme conflict and controversy over the proposed League of Nations. The gallery was packed when it was learned that Harding would be laying out his objections to the proposed legislation.

Dealing from the Bottom of the Deck

Robert acted as a go between and confidant to help secure the nomination for Warren Harding.

Poker at the Republican Convention: The Convention selects Warren Harding, June 12, 1920.

In the heat and intensity of Chicago, a smoke-filled room of politicians and promoters tried to establish which of the candidates would be selected on Saturday. With time running out and the candidates wanting to go home on Sunday, Harding was put forward as the choice.

It had been Harry Daughtery's, Harding's campaign manager's, plan to make Harding every delegate's second choice, and when neither General Wood, Governor Louden, nor Senator Johnson could gain a majority through seven ballots, Harding won the nomination. Warren Harding enjoyed playing poker. The poem uses poker as its theme for the nomination process.

It Was Cold on Inauguration Day and Thoughts on Inauguration Day

On Inauguration Day, President Wilson was a frail shell of what he had been. Agents of the Secret Service lifted him into the carriage and covered him with a blanket. Harding was in fine health.

Woodrow Wilson and president-elect Harding made a sharp contrast on the day Warren Harding took the oath of office. President Wilson was too weak to climb the stairs to the podium. Harding was in his prime, but he would be dead in two years.

★ ★ ★ ★

Calvin Coolidge

Calvin Coolidge had been selected as Harding's vice president. Harding had no interest in selecting a vice president. He left it up to the party bosses to name a candidate.

Coolidge had been governor of Massachusetts, but he was unknown on a national basis. The night Harding died while travelling on the west coast, Coolidge was visiting his parents in rural Vermont. He was awakened and took the oath of office on August 3, 1923, in the early-morning hours.

While he was president, the national economy boomed, which gave rise to widespread speculation in the equity and commodity markets. He was widely popular, but he saw a coming economic conflagration. He did not run for reelection. He issued a terse statement that he did not choose for reelection run in 1928.

Introduction

Robert finds stark contrasts between the terse comments and quiet demeanor of Coolidge and the loud excesses of the 1920s.

Middle of the Night in Plymouth Notch, Vermont

This sonnet describes what it was like for Coolidge to be awakened and then take the oath of office administered by his father.

Exegesis

This poem addresses Coolidge's terse way of responding to questions. His wife asked him what the minister had used for his theme at the Sunday service. His short answer was Sin.

The Business of America Is Business

In this ballade, Coolidge accepts the position held by his financial advisors that less government promotes liberty and a better environment for business. Personally, Coolidge was a model of restraint in the midst of a roaring economy and the jazz age of the 1920s.

Brevity

This poem captures the unresponsiveness and ungraciousness of Coolidge at a dinner party at the White House.

Advice on a Milk Bucket

Coolidge took his own advice when he sent out a brief message that he would not seek another term. He seemed to be hoping that he would be drafted, but it never happened.

The Coming Deluge

Corporate and personal debts were high. The nation was engaged in leveraging assets and reckless speculation. The party was coming to an end.

Introduction to the Next Six Presidents
(Hoover-Johnson)

Robert's son James succeeded him on the White House staff at the beginning of the Hoover administration. While Robert was respected by all he served and grew into a position of responsibility, James began as an apprentice in the transportation department where he worked on automobiles. Later, he worked in the kitchen and then moved into the communications center of the White House.

James kept possession of the old leather box and added to its contents. He collected poems when they became available and traveled with several presidents as a valet.

He accompanied Harry Truman on his railroad cross-country campaign. It was on the campaign train in Texas when he met Lyndon Johnson and Sam Rayburn. He admired Johnson and served as Johnson's informant during the Truman, Eisenhower, and Kennedy administrations.

The Old Man Continues Speaking

The Old Man who was sixty-four years old at the end of the Johnson administration recounts what it was like during the presidential years of Hoover through Johnson. James who worked for six presidents grew close to Lyndon Johnson during those years.

James Speaks of His Life in Washington and James's Sonnet: On His Retirement

James introduces his forty years serving six presidents. He then speaks of the importance of service.

****

Herbert Hoover

Herbert Hoover was born in Iowa and was a graduate of the first class of Stanford University with a degree in engineering. During World War I, he worked on food relief programs and later served as secretary of Commerce under presidents Harding and Coolidge. Even though he had never been elected to public office of any kind, Hoover won the Republican nomination in 1928.

Hoover believed in the responsibility of the individual, and when the crash of 1929 started the Great Depression, Hoover was blamed for it. Roosevelt defeated him in the election of 1932 and continued to blame him throughout the years Roosevelt was president.

Optimism reigned at the start of the Hoover presidency, but the Depression turned the country against him.

Fishing Stories

Early Morning on the Merced and on the **Russian River** detail Hoover's love of fishing and fishing stories.

Hoover fished the Russian River in California for Steelhead. A steelhead becomes a metaphor for Hoover's presidency.

Camping Beneath the Giant Sequoias

The Giant Sequoias of Northern California offered a place of invigoration and peace for Hoover and his associates. Camping there was inspirational for those fortunate to be in that environment.

Interregnum

This cynical poem lays out Roosevelt's strategy for making Hoover a continuing scapegoat. America was deeply divided. Long-standing friendships were lost over quarrels regarding Hoover and Roosevelt. Roosevelt preached class envy and class separation.

Living in a Hoover Hotel

This Depression-era folk song contrasts the joys of freedom with a downtrodden existence by many people in America during the Great Depression. It was a time of great dislocation and hardship. People often were forced to live under bridges, which became known as Hoover Hotels.

Musings while My Time Runs Out

At the end of his life, Hoover looked back at the presidents he knew, and he commented on them. His resentment of Roosevelt remained strong to the end. Truman invited him to the White House and treated him kindly.

Statism

Hoover's strong belief in the role of charity and responsibility of the individual lies at the heart of this poem. He feared that Socialism would destroy the American ideal.

* * * *

Franklin Roosevelt

Roosevelt defeated Hoover soundly and presided over the nation from 1933 until 1945. He came to power during the Great Depression and led the nation into World War II. He died in office as the war in Europe was coming to a conclusion. It was a tumultuous time, and the president was a popular, though polarizing figure for many.

Taking office, he launched a series of programs that came to be known as the New Deal. This expansion of the role of government was controversial. He was loved by most Americans, but he was hated by many.

Even though he as a paralyzed by polio in his late thirties, he conducted his affairs with an optimistic and energizing attitude.

Introduction

James survives the early days of Roosevelt and goes on to be a trusted helper for both Franklin and Eleanor.

Deception

Diagnosed with polio at the age of thirty-nine, Roosevelt lived a vigorous life even though his legs were paralyzed. With an amazing display of cunning and courage, he made sure the press never mentioned his paralysis or showed pictures of him in a wheel chair.

Revising the party

His plans for driving a wedge between mine owners and workers are explained by Roosevelt. He planned to make bankers the scapegoats for the country's problems.

My Plan to Expand the Court

As his plans ran afoul of the Supreme Court, Roosevelt sought to add Justices who would be favorable to his programs. He wanted to oust his opponents on the court and put in replacements who would vote his way.

Hirabayashi

After the Japanese bombed Pearl Harbor, Hawaii, Americans were paranoid of a potential invasion of the mainland. Thousands of Japanese Americans who lived on the west coast were relocated to internment camps. One of those camps was located in the Catalina Mountains near Tucson, Arizona. A young man from the state of Washington named Hirabayashi was forced to hitchhike to Tucson and live in the honor camp there. This Sonoran Desert Haiku commemorates that lost time.

Thoughts

This poem was written by a young woman in the internment camp near Heart Mountain in Wyoming. The author is unknown.

Correspondence, November 1940

Winston Churchill visited Roosevelt and corresponded with him frequently. Roosevelt was keeping America from joining the war in Europe. In this poem, Churchill pleads for America's direct help in the war with Germany. Roosevelt promises material support but makes no offer to send troops.

Enter Stage Left

Roosevelt had a great stage presence. Here he compliments himself for being a great political performer.

Save Me, God of Abraham

The poem poses the question, Where is God in the Nazi Death Camps? The Nazis systematically executed millions of people, and the man trudging toward the gas chamber asks God to save him.

1943

In 1943, Winston Churchill, Joseph Stalin and Roosevelt met to plan the war on Germany, and they met to discuss a postwar Europe. Roosevelt thought he captivated Stalin.

Lucy

Roosevelt had a long-term relationship with Lucy Mercer outside of his marriage. One of Roosevelt's wishes was that Lucy would be with him during his final days. Lucy was present with him as he was dying in Warm Springs, Georgia, in 1945. To avoid the press, Lucy was driven away.

A portrait of Roosevelt was being painted at the time of his death. The unfinished portrait became a popular print for those who wished to remember him.

Earlier Roosevelt's wife Eleanor had learned of his love for Lucy and offered Roosevelt a divorce, but Roosevelt's mother threatened to withdraw financial support for him if he got a divorce.

* * * *

Harry S. Truman

Truman was largely unknown at the time of Roosevelt's death in 1945. Truman had been a senator from Missouri when Roosevelt selected him to be his running mate in 1944. Truman had served in World War I and had seen military action.

At the time of Roosevelt's death, the war in Europe was winding down, but the war in the Pacific was far from ending. Truman made the decision to use nuclear weapons on the mainland of Japan in the belief he was saving countless American lives.

Following the end of the war, Truman faced a complicated set of issues. Domestically, the United States had to convert to a peacetime economy. Internationally, Russia and its allies were gaining strength in Europe. A Cold War was forming.

Behind in the polls in 1948, Truman made a bold move to take his case to the American people using a transcontinental rail trip. Crossing America via rail, Truman built support and won an upset victory over his Republican opponent, Tom Dewey.

Much of his second term was spent containing the Soviet Union and their allies. At home, he was subjected to scathing criticism.

Introduction

Mrs. Roosevelt dispatched James to fetch Truman to the White House to tell him the president was dead.

Menu for Sunday Lunch: Fried Chicken, Southern Biscuits, and Old Fashions

The Trumans set out to improve the quality of food coming from the White House kitchen. This poem was written by James based on conversations with the Trumans regarding how they wanted their Sunday lunch. They enjoyed fried chicken, biscuits, and old-fashions for Sunday lunch.

Justification

Truman had an angry meeting with a columnist over his decision to use nuclear weapons on mainland Japan. James stood outside the door and gave his notes to President Truman at the end of the meeting.

Rising and Falling in the Opinion Polls

Truman sank from being one of the most respected presidents when he first took office to one of the least respected presidents at the end. He thought that history would treat him favorably.

Salty Language in Independence

Truman would not pull punches for anyone. This lengthy poem contains his thoughts on everyone from J. Edgar Hoover to General Douglas MacArthur to Jack Kennedy. It was written after he was no longer in office.

The Whistle Stop Campaign

James was with Truman on this extended rail trip across the country. He took lengthy notes, and Truman put them into a long poem after the election. Truman was at his salty best and got stronger as the trip continued.

The tour ran out of funds in Oklahoma, and the train was sidetracked for several days until additional money could be raised. Lyndon Johnson and Sam Rayburn of Texas joined the train in San Antonio and were on the car when it stopped in Waco.

The trip caught the attention of the country, and it was a major factor in his victory.

* * * *

Dwight D. Eisenhower

A graduate of West Point, Eisenhower became a five-star general during World War II. After the war ended, Eisenhower served as president of Columbia University. He was nominated as the Republican candidate for president in 1952. His containment of the Soviet Union and the buildup of America's military strength during his presidential years are considered his greatest accomplishments.

Interests beyond the presidency included golf, painting and bridge. It was said that everyone on his staff needed to be good at bridge if he hoped for a promotion. He was a fair golfer and a good painter in his later years.

Introduction

Robert keeps his ears open for Lyndon Johnson during the Eisenhower presidency and provided information to Johnson. Johnson was the most powerful man in Washington for much of this time.

Ode to the Classes of 1915 and 1965

Officers of West Point celebrated fifty years of service by the class of 1915 and the commitment of the class of 1965. Eisenhower delivered this inspirational ode to them.

Nixon

Eisenhower did not care for his vice president. These notes were taken in a meeting with Republican Party officials.

Mentors

Eisenhower served on Conner, Pershing and MacArthur staffs. He did not like MacArthur, and the feeling was mutual.

Finesse the Queen

In Washington DC, during the war, four army wives met regularly to play bridge and share news and gossip. On this occasion, Mamie Eisenhower was not present.

End Play

At a cottage near London during the war, Eisenhower is host to a bridge game. The weather is cold, but the cottage is warm, and Eisenhower gets good cards.

An Airfield near London—June 5, 1945

On the eve of the Normandy invasion, Eisenhower contemplates the weather and the fate of his armada.

Unpacking for the Last Time

The lot of the life of an army wife is constant packing and unpacking during a military career. In this poem, Mamie Eisenhower enjoys the last time she has to unpack at their farm in Gettysburg, Pennsylvania.

Recalling My Life

Eisenhower met with an editor of a book of photographs of Eisenhower. The photographs produced a vivid sensory recall of past experiences.

* * * *

John F. Kennedy

No one candidate has ever captured the magic of John F. Kennedy's run for the presidency in 1960. He was the first serious Catholic candidate; he was handsome and vigorous; he had a large and interesting family, and he had a beautiful wife. He was educated and articulate, but he faced a strong candidate in Richard Nixon. It was a campaign that fascinated the nation, and it featured, for the first time, nationally televised debates between the candidates.

Kennedy won the presidency, only to be assassinated two years later. His assassination created a deep sadness in the country, launched numerous conspiracy theories, and brought Lyndon Johnson into the presidency.

James Speaks of John F. Kennedy

John Kennedy entered the White House at a time of sea change in America. The quiet generation of Americans was being replaced by a noisy, demanding generation.

A Visitor from Cambridge

A visitor to a seaside compound discusses with Kennedy books he is reading. Particularly comforting to Kennedy are St. Paul's letters, which show that suffering can lead to gratitude for things in life. The prospect of a storm overnight might cleanse the air and open up a better day.

Smoked Pork

Everyone seems to enjoy pork barrel legislation when it comes from a smoke filled room.

Pleasure Above the Abyss

Balanced on a personal tightrope can be exhilarating if the stakes are high and the risk is great. Kennedy enjoyed taking risks.

Joe Jr.

The star of the Kennedy siblings was Joseph Kennedy Jr. who died in World War II. This is a tribute from John Kennedy to his older brother Joe.

Ready to Debate in Chicago

The televised debates between Kennedy and Richard Nixon leading up to the presidential election were high theater for the country. Nixon was no match for Kennedy in the long run.

Ask Not, First Draft

This is the first draft of Kennedy's inauguration speech. It stirred the nation. The draft was recovered from the president's waste basket in the family quarters.

My New Attorney General

Kennedy's younger brother was appointed attorney general. He moved quickly against the Mafia and played tough with J. Edgar Hoover of the FBI.

For Sorenson, the "Nation's Son of Alliteration"

Ted Sorenson raised the tone and content of presidential speech making. Kennedy admired his contributions to the art.

A Dangerous World

Southeast Asia and Eastern Europe were hot spots for the new president. He did not accept isolation from these problems as a viable strategy.

The Window

Waiting patiently at the window of the Book Depository, time compresses for the assassin and instinct takes over.

Parkland

The Parkland Hospital Emergency Room was gruesome scene when the dying Kennedy was brought in. The day had started in Ft. Worth and ended in tragedy in Dallas, Texas.

An Unlocked Door

A desperate man assassinates Lee Oswald the perpetrator of the senseless act on John F. Kennedy.

* * * *

Lyndon Johnson

Lyndon Johnson was selected by John Kennedy to be his running mate as vice president over the objections of Bobby Kennedy and other Kennedy advisors. John Kennedy did not like Johnson, but he saw him as indispensable to help carry Texas and southern states.

Johnson had been a respected, feared leader in the senate. After the election, he lost considerable power and sources of information in the Oval Office. He recruited informants, and without much hesitation, James agreed to continue to provide information to Johnson. After Johnson became president, James gained more responsibility.

From Texas, Johnson never gained respect of the Eastern Establishment who considered him a political infighter. After he became president, Johnson became caught up in the nation's objection to the war in Vietnam. It was a war that could not be won, and it caused Johnson not to seek a second term of his own. His warmth for all people, rich or poor and black or white, has never been properly recognized.

Richard Nixon followed him to the White House, and Johnson retired to the Hill Country in Texas and took James with him. James drove Johnson from the ranch to Austin or San Antonio. When Johnson attended the State Fair in Dallas, James drove him there and waited in the car while Johnson attended the Oklahoma-Texas football game.

James Recounts His Days with Lyndon Johnson

James had a wealth of White House information that was useful to Johnson, and he kept him informed on rumors and appointments being considered.

Coffee at the Driskell Hotel

A guest lecturer at the Johnson Library and a guest panelist have breakfast at the Driskell Hotel in Austin to debate the pros and cons of Johnson's presidency.

Meeting President Roosevelt

President Roosevelt had been fishing in the Gulf of Mexico for tarpon and kingfish. He stopped in Galveston, Texas, and was introduced to a young politician named Lyndon Johnson.

Touring the Ranch

An evening cocktail tour at the Ranch turns deadly for a rusted tractor. James drove a Volkswagen bus and tended bar while Lyndon drove a white Lincoln.

Lyndon Is for the Little Guy

Johnson knew the concerns and fears of the people in rural areas of the country. He learned his lessons during the Depression and never forgot them.

Campaigning

Johnson liked a show when he was campaigning and was one of the first politicians to use a helicopter. After the helicopter landed, Johnson got out of the helicopter and rode slowly around the rodeo grounds in a white Lincoln convertible driven by James.

Big Tex at the State Fair

A political opponent of Lyndon's sent this poem to him after going to the State Fair in Dallas. James intercepted the poem and never showed it to Lyndon.

A Bitter End

Johnson was dealt a bad hand, and he did not do much to help himself with his approach to the war in Vietnam. Profoundly unhappy, he chose not to run. When he announced his decision, James cried.

Sunset

At the end of his life, Johnson wished he could roll back some of his life and change some things.

Introduction to the Poems of the Last Six Presidents

When James retired and followed Lyndon Johnson to Texas to live out his final days, he asked Johnson to ask Richard Nixon to appoint James's son John to a post in the White House. Nixon owed a few favors to Johnson and did so. John, son of James and grandson of Robert, carried on the family tradition and started on the day of Richard Nixon's inauguration. He traveled with Nixon on occasion as a valet. He went on to serve Gerald Ford by running errands and tending to guest's needs.

He stayed on during the Carter term and was demoted to kitchen duty, but with the arrival of the Reagans, John hit his stride. John helped with receptions and saw to guest's requirements. Then he stayed on with the Bush administration, and after Clinton won, he worked near the Oval Office doing whatever job was required. He traveled with Clinton, working in the back of *Air Force One* helping with appointments and correspondence.

At the end of the Clinton administration, John moved to New York and worked for a time in Clinton's office there. Then he took a job in the Clinton Library in Little Rock until he left to write a book on his experiences based on the poems collected by him, his father and grandfather.

The old leather box, which once belonged to Ulysses S. Grant, contained poems of all eighteen presidents and some memorabilia, which was given to the respective libraries of the presidents.

* * * *

Richard Nixon

Richard Nixon was the most polarizing president of the twentieth century. He served as a congressman, and he was vice president for eight years under Dwight Eisenhower. He was defeated in the presidential election of 1960 by John Kennedy. Controversy marked each of his steps along the way.

With his defeat by John Kennedy in 1960, he returned to California and later ran for governor. Again, he was defeated, and it appeared that he was finished as a national political figure. However, he returned to the national scene and won the presidency in 1968.

Entering office, Nixon faced a number of difficult international problems, but Nixon performed well and was elected for a second term. His administration began to unravel when it became known that he had authorized a break in of the Democratic Party headquarters in Washington DC. Calls for his impeachment caused him to resign the office, and Gerald Ford became president.

The Old Man Speaks for the Last Time

At the end of William Clinton's presidency in 2001, the Old Man celebrated his one-hundredth birthday. He reflects as best he can on the last six presidents of the twentieth century.

John Speaks of the Presidents His Grandfather and Father Served and John's Farewell

John has the advantage of having heard stories from his grandfather and father which he tells at the end of his tenure.

John asks us to say farewell to Nixon, Ford, Carter, Reagan, Bush and Clinton. Nixon was a complicated man. While he accomplished much while he was in office, Nixon became insulated and isolated, which caused him problems.

Rice Paddy

This poem was written by a soldier in Vietnam. The soldier is engulfed in the fog of war.

Mentors

No one ever helped Nixon much on the way up in life. At least, Nixon thought so. He saw himself as an outsider in life.

Despair

Losing the governor's race in California seemed to Richard Nixon that he was doomed as a political force.

Touchdown

His trademark salute was outspread arms over the head in a victory pose. He relished the sheer joy of the political arena.

The Chameleon's Gyroscope

Here Nixon attempts to answer what guides him as a politician. He will reflect a voter's desires. He concludes that he will be whatever the voter wants him to be.

Real Politick and Real Politics

Kissinger is pleased with his ability to manipulate Nixon. Nixon resented the presence of Henry Kissinger. Kissinger's ego offended him, even though Kissinger had an exceptional grasp of international affairs.

A Cautionary Note

His wife had discouraged him from seeking the presidency after his string of losses. This poem was found in a folder left behind after he resigned and departed the White House.

Agony

Everyone abandoned him during the Watergate hearings. The political posse had run him down. He thinks his presidency has been stolen from him.

* * * *

Gerald Ford

Ford was a respected congressman who was appointed vice president after Spiro Agnew was forced to resign. He was not Nixon's first choice.

After Nixon resigned in disgrace, Ford faced a difficult decision. Should Nixon be prosecuted for his acts while he was in office, or should Ford pardon him to end the continuing distraction and national debate? Ford chose to pardon Nixon, and many say it cost him any chance for reelection.

Between a Rock and a Hard Place and
My Reason to Pardon Nixon Now

The pardon of Nixon by Ford created a storm of controversy. Ford was sure he could govern effectively once the pardon controversy died down.

Stagflation

The combination of rising prices and high unemployment bedeviled the Ford administration. His program of Whip Inflation Now did little to relieve the problem. It was nothing more than a slogan.

Dealing with Assassination Plots

Ford reflects on the danger of assassination attempts. He would face two close encounters during his presidency.

Her Breast Cancer

Ford's wife Betty raised the consciousness of American women to issues of breast cancer. Openly acknowledging her treatment helped advance women's health issues.

I Enjoy Smoking My Pipe

Ford was never far from his favorite pipes and tobacco. Smoking was becoming a national health issue at the time.

* * * *

Jimmy Carter

Jimmy Carter had been governor of Georgia and won the presidency based on an ineffective campaign by Gerald Ford and the desire of the American people to put the entire Watergate controversy behind them. Carter presided during a difficult time of energy shortages. American hostages were held by the Iranian government.

He made the mistake of asking the American people to make sacrifices such as not overheating their homes. He wore a sweater as a symbol to the nation. The American people did not want to make sacrifices and voted against what they perceived as weak leadership.

Carter accomplished many good things during his time in office, but Ronald Reagan made Carter out to be the symbol of a weakening nation.

In Defense of President Carter

This poem is a rigorous defense of Carter's administration. It concludes that Carter was damaged by Ted Kennedy's backers who wanted Kennedy to replace Carter in the presidential election. John was given a copy of this poem after Carter had moved back to Georgia.

The author of this poem is unknown, but it is probably Hamilton Jordan.

A South Georgia Evening

The Milky Way in all its majesty is above South Georgia. Carter thinks about his purpose in life and devotes himself to a life of peace and justice. This poem was given to John by Carter when he was moving out of the White House.

When Hell Reached for Heaven

When Mt. St. Helen exploded, it caused devastation to plants and animals in the Pacific Northwest. Even though an eruption was thought to be imminent, no one was prepared for the destruction that followed.

Saturday Brunch, Listening to the Football Game

As a peanut farmer, Carter offered up dishes based on peanuts while the Georgia football games were broadcast on the radio. John learned to make peanut brittle and became accomplished at it. The White House chef never made peanut dip correctly, so Carter removed it from the White House buffet.

Extended Political Families

Carter's large extended family and a network of friends and advisors helped him along the way in his quest for office. John served all of them when they were guests in the White House and kept a beer box replenished for Carter's extended family.

Babe Ruth and Hank Aaron in Their Prime

This mathematical fantasy explores the nature of prime numbers as it relates to the day Hank Aaron broke Babe Ruth's home record. Observing the action from Ted Turner's box and attempting to reconcile the proof are Ted Turner, owner of the Braves, guests David Forney, a baseball statistics expert, Paul Erdos, a famous mathematician, and Rosalyn and Jimmy Carter. The poem asks if 1429 is a number of baseball magic and subtly inquires if the reader has an Erdos number. John listened to the game on the radio in the car and drove Erdos back to his hotel after the game. Erdos offered to get Hank Aaron an Erdos number of one, but he never followed through.

The *Jimmy Carter* at Rest in Kipsap, Washington

A Sea Wolf class nuclear submarine was named in honor of Jimmy Carter.

Early Fall on the Madison

Carter and his wife, Rosalyn, fly fished on the Madison River. Presentation of the fly required exceptional skill. Occasionally, John helped the president practice at Camp David.

Frozen Images

Images of his days in office formed the foundation for his work through the Carter Center in Atlanta.

* * * *

Ronald Reagan

Ronald Reagan was a gifted communicator and an engaging speaker who delighted his audiences. His acting experience and television appearances helped him in California when he was governor and then when he ran for the president. He and George Bush seemed incompatible during the Republican primary in 1980, but Reagan selected him as his vice presidential running mate.

The ticket overwhelmingly defeated Jimmy Carter and won a landslide victory for reelection four years later.

Reagan was old for the office of president, but his optimism and trust in the American people carried the day over his political opponents. He survived an assassination attempt and went on to attempt to limit the size of government in a meaningful way.

His view was to keep pressure on the Soviet Union and engage in direct personal talks with Soviet Premier Mikhail Gorbachev.

When Reagan left office, he returned to California, confident he had made the nation a better place.

Dear Diary

Reagan kept meticulous notes and diaries during his time in office. This is a copy of one of his entries he gave to John.

At the Movies

Movie titles comprise a poem made for Reagan's enjoyment. He enjoyed watching the movies even though they were B movies for the most part.

Campaigning with Five by Seven Cards

Reagan made effective use of a set of five by seven cards with notes and instructions. John's job was to keep them in order during Reagan's run for a second term.

Commencement

At West Point, Reagan offered advice to the next generation of leaders.

Détente

Reagan put an end to a too lengthy discussion on diplomatic alternatives for Russia in this poem. He knew what he wanted.

Assassination Attempts

The real threat of an assassination attempt by a deranged killer was a real possibility. Reagan survived an attempt on his life.

Cargo

Shadow support for the Contras in Central America caused great embarrassment for the Reagan administration

A Rainbow of Scents

Hay, sweat and leather were a background for the smell of breakfast cooking at the Reagan ranch in California.

J. Peter Grace Reports

Reagan recruited Peter Grace, who was a Democrat, to lead a private sector effort on cost control of the government. Grace in turn recruited a large number of private sector executives whom he organized and set to work in Washington.

Today's Horoscope

Nancy Reagan relied on several astrologers over the years. This poem contains a warning from one of them. John extracted it from a trash bin at the White House and kept it in the old leather box.

My Lucky Stars

Joan Quigley, an astrologer, Nancy Reagan and Donald Regan, Reagan's chief of staff, weigh in on their viewpoints toward each other. Nancy Reagan embarrassed the White House when it was learned that she consulted astrologers. She did not like Regan at all. Regan was pushed out and took some verbal shots at Nancy Reagan to the delight of the press after he departed.

Evening at Rancho del Cielo

Senses are heightened at Rancho del Cielo following a day of physical work.

Gentle Rain

Alzheimer's disease is the curse of Reagan's generation. The suspension and loss of time and memory rob many victims.

* * * *

George H. W. Bush

Before becoming vice president under Reagan for two terms, Bush had a long career of public service, as a congressman from Texas, as director of Central Intelligence, as ambassador to the United Nations, as head of the Republican Party and as an envoy to China.

    Bush was a navy pilot in World War II, and after the war was over, he returned from the Pacific and graduated from Yale where he played baseball. Rather than following his father's path to Wall Street, he chose to move to Texas and sell oil field supplies.

Eventually he started his own gulf drilling company and was successful at an early age. John got to know Bush during his eight years as vice president. When Bush became president, John continued to work in the White House.

George H. W. Bush

John describes how he knew Bush and what he thought of him. He calls him a man of unquestioned veracity.

Because It Is the Right Thing to Do

Prescott Bush, George's father, instilled a code of conduct in his son. George lived by these words and passed them on to his children.

The Day They Brought Down the Chichi Jima Tower—A Ballad

Flying from a carrier in World War II, George Bush dive-bombed a communications tower on an island in the Pacific. In the action, his plane was hit and crashed into the ocean where he floated in a raft until he was rescued by a submarine. He was decorated for his brave action.

Betrayal

Bush was between a rock and a hard place as Nixon fought to keep his job because of the Watergate scandal. Bush had been defending Nixon to the Congress and to his own party because Nixon had assured Bush that he knew nothing about the break in. As chairman of the Republican Party, Bush did everything he could to defend Nixon.

Then he read an account in the *Washington Post* that directly implicated Nixon in the scandal. Wasting no time, Bush composed a letter requesting that Nixon resign. Bush took it to Nixon and laid it on the line: Nixon must resign. This poem was written immediately prior to Bush's meeting with Nixon. John retrieved it from the trash bin.

First Base

The joy of college competition on the baseball diamond comes through in this poem written when Bush was playing first base for Yale.

Seeking Lyndon's Advice on the Senate Race

Secretly Lyndon Johnson agreed to support Bush for the senate against Ralph Yarborough, the Democrat. However, if Lloyd Benson won the Democratic primary, Lyndon would support Benson.

My Favorite Par Three

George Bush was a very good golfer. In this poem, he reflects on great par threes in the world and selects Pine Valley number 10 as his favorite.

Rhetorical Questions

In this poem, the techniques of rhetoric are applied to issues that the Republicans and George Bush faced. The first time, I was afraid to run for office. The last time, I was afraid not to run for office is an example of symploce, a rhetorical technique.

Thoughts on a Winter Day by Mildred Kerr Bush

In the White House, Millie, the Bush's Springer Spaniel, had free run of many of the rooms. Millie discusses her preferences for names. Then Millie is launched outside by Barbara Bush to chase a squirrel away from the back porch.

Irony

Bush received this poem from Mikhail Gorbachev reflecting on the ending of the cold war. Off the Coast of Maine George Bush was most relaxed when he was in his powerboat off the coast of Maine. He learned the waters at a young age and was a competent boatman.

* * * *

William Jefferson Clinton

When Bill Clinton defeated George Bush, John was wary of the new arrivals from Arkansas. Whereas the Bush family was disciplined, he had heard that the Clintons worked all the time and at odd hours. What he had heard was correct, so from the start, the routines of the White House were turned upside down. Schedules were no longer etched in stone. Instead, schedules were treated as targets that need not be met with any consistency.

It did not take long for John to enjoy being in the same house as the Clintons. They were demanding, vital, and full of energy. He gravitated to the president and worked hard for him.

The Clintons were secretive on many subjects, and as John gained their confidence, they shared many personal opinions with him. When they left office, Clinton gave John a folder containing poems. Clinton kept another folder for himself.

John resigned when Clinton left office and moved to New York to work in Clinton's office. Later, he moved to Little Rock and worked in the Clinton Library.

Thinking About William Jefferson Clinton

John was intrigued with Clinton's intellect and insight.

Wedding Day

On his wedding day, Bill Clinton wrote this sonnet to a friend.

My Strategy

Clinton lays out his strategy to defeat George H. W. Bush for president.

We Will Govern as Equal Partners

Clinton thought of his wife, Hillary, as an equal partner in governing. It got him in trouble with the voters in Arkansas when he was governor, and it got him in trouble early in his first term in Washington.

Complete the Nominations

Clinton and his advisors could not complete his nominations for various posts in a timely manner. Here he is chided for a lack of disciplined action.

Get the Press off My Back

Clinton blamed George Stephanopoulos for his bad relationships with the press. Unable to see that he might have made some bad decisions, he let Stephanopoulos have an earful.

Tactic to Conclude Dayton Negotiations

Negotiations at Dayton regarding Sarajevo were not progressing, so Clinton's man on the scene sent this report back to the White House.

Reaction to the State of the Union Speech, Delivered on January 24, 1995

Clinton was joyous from the national reactions to his speech. He tells Dick Morris that he hit it out of the park.

Here Comes the '94 Midterms

Clinton hired Dick Morris as an advisor from Little Rock days. Under the code name Charlie, Morris insisted that Clinton remain off the campaign trail during the 1994 midterms, or the party would lose seats.

You Are Dead Wrong, Charlie

Clinton predicts victory for the Democrats. He should have listened to Charlie.

We Lost the Midterms

Charlie was right, but he reports the facts and does not gloat.

Spring House Cleaning After the Midterms

After his party's defeat and being swept from power after the first two years of the Clinton administration, Clinton thinks through what he has to do to be crowned the Comeback Kid for a second time.

A Day of Horror

The Oklahoma bombing was a senseless act of two men who felt the government had overstepped its authority at Ruby Ridge and Mt. Carmel interventions. It was a terrible act of terrorism.

Death of a Rock and Roll Prophet

Early in Clinton's term, federal agents crashed into the Branch Davidian compound near Waco, Texas. In the ensuing fire, many inside were burned to death. John had been sent there as an unidentified observer and sent this report back.

Ode for a Fallen Warrior

Yitzhak Rabin was assassinated in Tel Aviv, and Clinton went to the memorial taking John and others on *Air Force One*. John was assigned to watch Newt Gingrich, speaker of the House, who was given a seat near the back of the plane. Newt thought he was not being treated with respect and complained loudly all the way back to Washington.

A Lesson from Judges

Clinton made some bad choices and pleads with God to send him counsel who can show him a way out of his trouble.

Five Frozen Margaritas, No Salt

Mexico was in a financial crisis. Clinton moved quickly to rescue it on the advice of Robert Rubin.

Thank You for Your Service

Clinton acknowledged John's service of eight years and gives him a folder of poems.

In Case You Think I Am Leaving

Clinton vows to help Hillary Clinton to the presidency.

* * * *

ACKNOWLEDGMENTS
The author has many to thank for this work.

Dulcy Brainard for her encouragement and strategic direction,
Bruce Johnston for his insightful paintings,
Carole Magnuson for managing the documents,
David Forney for his help on the Mathematical Garden,
Robert Snyder for research, design, and publishing,
Jeff Ross for listening,
Edward Murphy for his haiku contribution.
Wilmette, Illinois, Public Library for research assistance.
Mitch Engel for his guidance.

The Author

John Kermit Kerr has enjoyed working on this collection of poems for a decade. When he first started on this work, he thought he might write eighteen sonnets, one for each president of the twentieth century, in three months. Things got out of hand quickly, but he has enjoyed the journey. Along the way, he has met interesting people and made new friends as a result of this work.

Born in Texas, he graduated from Baylor University. He spent most of his working career in the health care information systems business. Midcareer, he worked as project manager of the Computer Task force of the Grace Commission. He lives in

Tucson, Arizona, with his wife of fifty-four years. He has children in Oregon and Illinois and two grandchildren.

The Artist

R. Bruce Johnston is a registered architect and self-taught oil painting artist. His fifty-plus years of combined background in architecture and planning has molded his design philosophy as it applies to art and has given him unique perspective from a widely diverse professional experience. He is licensed in states in the Midwest and Southwest and has worked nationally and in Europe. Besides architectural illustration, his art includes landscape, figurative and portraiture in oil, charcoal, and watercolor.